LAW, CRIME AND LAW ENFORCEMENT

# LAW ENFORCEMENT AND CRIME

# LAW, CRIME AND LAW ENFORCEMENT

Additional books in this series can be found on Nova's website under the Series tab.

Additional e-books in this series can be found on Nova's website under the e-book tab.

LAW, CRIME AND LAW ENFORCEMENT

# LAW ENFORCEMENT AND CRIME

EMANUEL T. RHODES
EDITOR

nova publishers
*New York*

**Library of Congress Cataloging-in-Publication Data**

Names: Rhodes, Emanuel T., author.
Title: Law enforcement and crime / editor, Emanuel T. Rhodes.
Description: Hauppauge, New York : Nova Science Publishers, Inc., [2016] | Series: Law, crime and law enforcement | Includes index.
Identifiers: LCCN 2015041001 (print) | LCCN 2015044840 (ebook) | ISBN 9781634841276 (hardcover) | ISBN 9781634841283 ()
Subjects: LCSH: Criminology--United States. | Crime--United States. | Law enforcement--United States.
Classification: LCC HV6789 .L39 2016 (print) | LCC HV6789 (ebook) | DDC 364.973--dc23
LC record available at http://lccn.loc.gov/2015041001

*Published by Nova Science Publishers, Inc. † New York*

# CONTENTS

# PREFACE

This book provides an overview of current analyses and developments pertaining to the law enforcement and crime. Chapter one analyzes individual elements of the polygraph examination in pre-employment cases in law enforcement agencies, and attempts to answer the following questions: How are existing standards "scientific"? What should be done to raise the level of quality control in this kind of examinations? Chapter two studies the use of insects as evidence and as a forensic indicator in law enforcement technology. Chapter three explores a public health approach to preventing child fatalities. Chapter four discusses the prospects of the use of prison informers. Chapter five studies the homicide rates in the U.S. and their correlation with other publicly available data applying this nonstandard visualization technique; and a comparison of homicide rates in the U.S. to that of different Latin American countries is shown. The last chapter is an attempt to show that violence in American popular culture can be justified, and may even serve the story. The chapter will focus on depicting concrete scenes from Paul Verhoeven's 1987 film Robocop to prove that apart from showing violence, they actually raise important sociological and psychological matters.

Chapter 1 – In scientific literature relatively little space is devoted to issues of "scientificity" of polygraph examinations in pre-employment matters in law enforcement agencies. The authors of this chapter treat the feature of "scientificity" not as dichotomous but as a gradable one. The method of research in the field of forensic science may thus be more or less scientific depending on two of its features: the degree of support of methodology standards based on the results of empirical research and the degree of knowledge of its error area. In the context of the current discussion regarding the use of "research culture" elements in the field of forensic science it is worth looking into the issue of "scientificity" of polygraph examinations in pre-employment matters. The feature of "scientificity" is associated with its susceptibility to control (at least on the part of another expert) and transparency of an examination. The aim of the authors is both to analyze the individual elements of the polygraph examination in pre-employment cases in law enforcement agencies (what this examination is like in the practice, with reference mainly to the Polish practice), and to attempt to answer the following questions: How are existing standards "scientific"? What should be done to raise the level of quality control in this kind of examinations?

Chapter 2 – In recent years, criminal justice system necessitates the coordination of multidisciplinary professionals such as investigators, magistrates and scientists. Forensic entomology is in practice ever since the thirteenth century, and remains as one of the key scientific tools ensuring precision for medico-legal and criminal investigations. It includes the collection, documentation, preservation and analysis of insects and other arthropods as evidences in the legal context. It is mainly employed to determine the elapsed time since death [Postmortem interval; (PMI)] in case of suspicious death, e.g., homicide and suicide investigations by inferring with various both abiotic and biotic parameters like entomological evidence, geoclimaticdata, location and condition of the corpse, etc.

Indeed cadaverous critters provide decisive clues about a crime by estimating the age of the oldest necrophagous insects that developed on the corpse, or by analyzing the insect species composition on the corpse. Two major groups of insect's viz., Dipterans (True flies/Mosquitoes/ Gnats/Midges) and Coleopterans (beetles) are primarily used as forensic indicators. Carrion entomofauna analysis as a forensic tool has acquired more recognition as the blow flies (*Diptera: Calliphoridae*) and flesh flies (*Diptera: Sarchophagidae*) are the first creatures to locate and colonize the cadavers within ten-minutes of demise. Interestingly, they are capable of sensing corpse from as far as ten-miles away. Many insect species are engaged at each stage of carcass decomposition. Arthropod succession patterns and developmental rates of succession entomofauna enable effective investigation, if the murderee has been dead for a month or longer.

Entomological evidences are often more accurate and sometimes the only scientifically reliable forensic technique of estimating PMI, which subsequently could lead to death probe. It is equally helpful in determining the circumstances of abuses and sexual-molestation too. Besides, it is extremely useful in various steps of investigation like; (1) estimating the time of death, (2) movement of the corpse, (3) manner and cause of demise, (4) create a link between perpetrator and suspect with the death scene, and (5) detection of toxins, drugs, or even the DNA of the victim through molecular analysis of insect samples. It often validates the identity of a victim too. However, the significance of forensic entomology is often undermined or overlooked in the emerging economies due to lack of resources and skilled professionals. Therefore, adequate forensic entomology laboratory facilities must be set up in each province as there is a great need for research in order to assist the criminal justice system in the near future.

Chapter 3 – A child fatality is the death of a child caused by an injury resulting from abuse or neglect or where abuse or neglect was a contributing factor. It is estimated that there were 1,520 childhood deaths from abuse and neglect in the USA in 2013. Most victims are infants and the perpetrators are usually parents acting singly or together. A public health approach is likely to address the problem and involves four fundamental activities: (1) the surveillance of the injury; (2) identification of its risk factors and protective factors; (3) evaluation of interventions that reduce the injury burden and (4) dissemination and widespread adoption of best practices that are effective in decreasing the burden of injury. Child fatalities are an important but under-recognized problem related to under-reporting, lack of consistent standards for child autopsies, varying roles and inadequate coordination of Child Protective Service agencies and investigating agencies and a lack of training of medical examiners in child abuse and neglect. Prevention of child fatalities requires a multidisciplinary, comprehensive approach that looks at data, takes action and promotes policy changes at the federal, state and local levels with the active engagement of families and their communities.

Chapter 4 – This chapter is devoted to cooperation between police forces and personal sources of information, recognized as one of the most important methods of operational work. The necessity of taking corrective actions in this area in Poland has been noticed for many years because, without efficiently functioning network of informants, it is difficult to imagine the effective implementation of operational actions for example those ones against organized crime groups. An important part in this system can be prison informants who collect information from detainees in detention centers or prisons. This category of sources has not been analyzed yet, and there is no doubt that penitentiary institutions can be a source of valuable knowledge about various crime groups. It may concern for instance illegal contacts between criminals, their attempts to affect the course of criminal processes or their managing criminal activities by inmates coming from organized crime groups. Prison informants, however, are perceived very negatively in Poland, which is certainly influenced by past experience. Apart from this, there are a lot of difficulties connected with the cooperation with personal sources of information and the lack of appropriate regulations. Thus, nowadays, there are few perspectives of collecting valuable knowledge from prison informants in a large scale.

Chapter 5 – In general, the collection of statistical data at local, regional or national level requires extensive funding that is provided by different organizations. These data are collected in large tables and used for different purposes by many entities. It is difficult to relate data by simple inspection of the tables. Consequently, it is worth representing these data on elegant maps that are useful and easily readable. The visualization method used for the construction of these maps is based on ideas from elementary physics. The regular map regions are rescaled to be proportional to statistical values of each region, so the statistical density on the rescaled map is homogeneously distributed. The method allows one to choose a balance between good density equalization and low distortion of map regions. We study the homicide rates in the U.S. and their correlation with other publicly available data applying this nonstandard visualization technique. Finally, a comparison of homicide rates in the U.S. to that of different Latin American countries is shown.

Chapter 6 – This chapter is an attempt to show that violence in American popular culture can be justified, and may even serve the story. What is to be analyzed in the given text is Paul Verhoeven's 1987 film Robocop. This essay will focus on depicting concrete scenes, and proving that apart from showing violence, they actually raise important sociological and psychological matters.

In: Law Enforcement and Crime
Editor: Emanuel T. Rhodes
ISBN: 978-1-63484-127-6


*Chapter 1*

# ON THE ISSUE OF PRE-EMPLOYMENT POLYGRAPH EXAMINATIONS IN LAW ENFORCEMENT AGENCIES

***Piotr Herbowski[1,*] and Marek Leśniak[2]***
[1]Assistant Professor, Department of Criminal Law, Faculty in Poznań, University of Social Sciences and Humanities, Poznań, Poland
[2]Assistant Professor, Department of Criminalistics, Faculty of Law and Administration, University of Silesia in Katowice, Poland

## ABSTRACT

In scientific literature relatively little space is devoted to issues of "scientificity" of polygraph examinations in pre-employment matters in law enforcement agencies. The authors of this chapter treat the feature of "scientificity" not as dichotomous but as a gradable one. The method of research in the field of forensic science may thus be more or less scientific depending on two of its features: the degree of support of methodology standards based on the results of empirical research and the degree of knowledge of its error area. In the context of the current discussion regarding the use of "research culture" elements in the field of forensic science it is worth looking into the issue of "scientificity" of polygraph examinations in pre-employment matters. The feature of "scientificity" is associated with its susceptibility to control (at least on

* Corresponding author: Piotr Herbowski, PhD. E-mail: piotr.herbowski@wp.pl.

the part of another expert) and transparency of an examination. The aim of the authors is both to analyze the individual elements of the polygraph examination in pre-employment cases in law enforcement agencies (what this examination is like in the practice, with reference mainly to the Polish practice), and to attempt to answer the following questions: How are existing standards "scientific"? What should be done to raise the level of quality control in this kind of examinations?

**Keywords:** polygraph examination, law enforcement agencies, forensic science, scientific standards

## INTRODUCTION

The development of forensic sciences was connected with an issue of "scientificity" of methods developed in particular areas of these sciences. This matter originally played an important role in the field of a criminal trial. In some countries, for example in the USA, the acknowledgement of the methodology applied by an expert as "scientific" resulted in the limitation of the possibility of the jury to question evidence obtained this way. According to Frey's standards that have been used in the USA since 1923 as a scientific methodology can be recognized only the one which is based on a sufficiently established theory. What is more, it should be accepted in this field of science where it was formed (Memon, Vrij and Bull 2003). Then, with an increasing use of methodologies created for a criminal trial purpose beyond such a trial, the issue of "scientificity" of the methodology in an activity of various state services or business organizations (Herbowski 2010) also arose in non-trial areas. The purpose of our chapter is to draw attention to various problems in the context of the use of polygraph examinations for recruitment purposes in different kinds of state services. So, the question arises whether in the context of the use of different kinds of methodologies within state services, especially polygraph examinations, the issue of "scientificity" of these methodologies plays a significant role. Are there any premises to favor the "scientific" methodologies in relation to other ones? We must remember that these days pre-employment polygraph examinations are extensively conducted in state services of numerous countries worldwide, in fact, on all continents except The Antarctic (Krapohl 2002). In the USA the polygraph examinations for such purposes were conducted as early as 1995 by 99 big and 90 small agencies that were involved in controlling law compliance (Krapohl 2002; Pasko-Porys 2007).

## SCIENTIFICITY OF METHODOLOGY

Nowadays, in many countries, the so-called Dubert's standards with their modifications are taken into account in terms of scientificity of the methodology. They are the standards formed in the field of a specific American trial, however, there are some references to them in the world literature and they are claimed to be universal. According to Ch. W. Daniels (2002) to ascertain whether the methodology is 'scientific' the following issues are taken into consideration:

- If the theory, which the theory is based on, is susceptible to empirical testing,
- If an external accuracy of the methodology is known (we know how often we make mistakes when we apply correctly the specific methodology),
- If the methodology or the theory, which this methodology is based on, are described in the reviewed scientific publications,
- To which degree the methodology or the theory, which this methodology is based on, are accepted in a scientific community,
- In what scope the standards which determine acceptable use of this methodology exist.

We share the opinion of J. Konieczny elaborated in the context of the Dubert's standards that, above all, two features determine the level of "scientificity" of a particular methodology. They are such features as the level of its standardization and the level of knowledge of an error area of this methodology. The issue of the level of the methodology standardization is not only related to the level of standardization of the methodology in general, but also to the issue how the applied standards of examinations of are based on the results of empirical research. In the process of the development of forensic sciences there is a tendency to pass from methodologies based on generalizations derived from everyday experience to methodologies based on empirical generalizations, that is, the results of empirical research. The size of an error area of findings made with the help of the specific methodology is possible to assess thanks to ongoing empirical research, both in the form of empirical experiments and also in relation to the use of the methodology in real cases. The feature of "scientificity" of the methodology should not be regarded as a divalent feature but as a gradable one (Konieczny 2010). Therefore, the methodology can be more or less scientific depending on to what extent it is standardized and to what extent the applicable standards are based on empirical research (methodologically correct). It is worth noting that the existence of standards in the application of a specific methodology generally enables the supervision of an expert's work. Such a supervision involves a comparison of what the expert did with what he should do in the light of accepted standards. The lack of standards or their excessive vagueness does not allow for any control of the expert's work. This also concerns the pre-employment polygraph examinations. In every state service where such examinations are carried out detailed and appropriately formulated standards must exist. The level of scientificity of the methodology also depends on the knowledge level of its error area. Thus, as far as the pre-employment polygraph examinations used in state services are concerned, the level of their "scientificity" depends on the above mentioned elements. The answer to the following question seems indispensable: How important is the application of "scientific" methods in state services? Certainly, the most important feature of methodologies is their transparency, susceptibility of one expert's conclusions to a control carried out by another expert.

As mentioned above, it depends on the level of standardization of the methodology. This is what makes the quality management of some examinations possible. It is in the interest of both the subjects ordering such examinations and employing the candidates who will successfully pass the recruitment process and in the interest of the verified candidates. The former ones do not want to employ, for example, a person who has ties with foreign intelligence or criminal organizations (Cempura, Kasolik and Widacki 2014) but the person having appropriate qualifications (the result of the polygraph examination can, after all, justify a wrong thesis that such a person has ties with criminal organizations). On the other hand, in the interest of the examinee is the confirmation that he had not committed acts unwanted by the prospective employer. The mistakes made by a polygrapher may result in losing by the examinee the possibility of fulfilling his professional aspirations or worsening his standard of living. Therefore, we believe that the quality of polygraph examinations conducted on people who want to be employed in state services should be a subject to equally strict control as the quality of examinations conducted for evidentiary purposes in criminal proceedings (Gołaszewski 2013; Herbowski and Słapczyńska 2015).

## Unification of Legal Regulations

The discourse on the quality of polygraph examination we embed in a descriptive area. Nevertheless, the issue of the standardization of pre-employment polygraph examinations can be considered in the context of both the normative area and also legal regulations involving various issues related to conducting the polygraph examinations. Should there be shared legal regulations regarding the pre-employment polygraph examinations for all services operating in the country? Should any service, taking into account its objectives and the peculiarities of its operation, have its own legislation in this regard? Generally, any polygraph examination must be in accordance with existing law. It must be consistent with the constitution and other acts. In Poland the polygraph examinations are currently carried out in many services each of which has its own legal regulation concerning polygraph examinations included in the act regulating the operation of such a service (Wójcikiewicz 2004; Zubańska 2010). They are as follows: the Police (Article 35 of the Police Act of 6 April, 1990), the Military Intelligence and Counterintelligence Services (Article 5.2 of the Act of June, 2006 on the Military Intelligence Service and Counterintelligence Service), the Border Guard (Article 31.1a paragraph 5 of the Act of 12 October,1999 on the Border Guard), the Central Anti-Corruption Bureau (Article 50.2 of the Act of June, 2006 on the Central Anti-Corruption Bureau), the Internal Security Agency and the Intelligence Agency (Article 46.2 of the Act of 24 May, 2002 on the Internal Security Agency and the Intelligence Agency), the Customs Service (Article 102.1 of the Act of 27 August, 2009 on the Customs Service), the Military Police (Article 9.1a of the Act of 24 August, 2001 on the Military Service and the Military Law Enforcement Authorities). The content of each of those regulations varies in:

- The degree of exactness of the examination procedure description,
- The way of the description of posts that require conducting the examination when applying for them,
- Pointing out the polygraph examination as compulsory for all officers or candidates for officers and making the conduct of such examinations independent from the decision of the superior,
- The consequences of the refusal to participate in the examination,
- The various consequences of the negative for the candidate results of the polygraph examination.

In our opinion, a certain unification of legal regulations concerning the conduct of the pre-employment polygraph examinations in state services in Poland is required. It is also necessary to define precisely the role of the result of the polygraph examination in the whole of recruiting new employees of state services. In some services this examination has only a psychological effect to discourage the candidates, whose curriculum vitae does not meet the employing services expectations, from applying for a specific post or to lead to disclosing their "sins" already in the course answering the pre-test questions which precede the relevant polygraph examination (Wiśniewski 2005). In the case of an unfavorable for the candidate result of the examination it is not precisely defined how significant it is to take the final decision whether or not to hire a particular person. This makes the whole process of recruitment non-transparent. In the scientific literature it is noted that the pre-employment polygraph examination is only part of the recruitment process (Krapohl 2002) and is used most often to obtain information inaccessible from other sources (Wiśniewski 2005).

It is worth noting that, similarly to the situation in Poland, also in American services the process of using information obtained in the polygraph examination during the recruitment is diverse (Krapohl 2002). In the opinion of the authors of this publication, ethical considerations require to inform the candidate for work in a specific service, how much the polygraph examination result influenced rejecting his application in the process of recruitment (Leśniak 2008). To check the quality of this kind of examinations the positive effect would probably have the legal possibility of such a person (or his lawyers) to initiate a control of the examination by an expert working in a different service than the one who conducted the pre-employment examination.

## Standardization of Pre-Employment Polygraph Examinations

The pre-employment polygraph examinations usually consist of three components such as responding by the subject to the questionnaire questions (this phase is not connected with the registration of psychophysiological reactions of the subject), the polygraph examination and the post-test interview when the results of the test are discussed with the subject. The standardization of the polygraph examination should concern above all:

- The way of conducting the test before the polygraph examination as well as the content of questionnaire questions;
- The way of choosing and the content of the questions used in polygraph examinations (for example, as concerns the control questions tests this issue includes a selection of the control questions);
- The way of disclosing the so-called "artifacts" (the various kinds of disturbances occurring in the course of the polygraph examination);
- The polygrapher's reaction to various situations which can arise during the examination (for example, the subject's behavior, the polygrapher's behavior, intrusion into the room where the examination takes place, etc.);
- The way of registration of the subject's psychophysiological reactions;
- The way of the measurement of the prominence of the psychophysiological reactions;
- The way of interpretation of the examination results (it is very important to use numerical or quasi-numerical scales when interpreting) (Słapczyńska 2013);
- The way of archiving the conducted examination.

In Polish state services, however, different standards are applied in respect of the examination conduct, the interpretation of its results, archiving the materials from the examination, reacting in the case of the unfavorable for the subject results of the examination.

In Poland, interdepartmental meetings of officers of various state services are held each year aimed at exchanging their experience and working on the common standards for polygraph examinations. Such meetings are primarily organized by the Headquarters of the Military Police, the Internal Security Agency and also the Police Academy in Szczytno (Gołaszewski 2011). The scientists who are concerned with the polygraph examinations are also invited there. Certainly, this is a great opportunity to exchange experience. However, we are quite skeptical as far as the significance of the past meetings to unify the standards of polygraph examinations in Poland is concerned.

The problem that may occur (more often in the case of the periodic loyalty polygraph examinations) is the hierarchical link between the polygrapher and the examinee in particular, the polygrapher should not be subordinate to the examined person. Then, there is a serious risk (even if the examination is archived properly) that this examination will be carried out too routinely.

There are some publications where the standards of pre-employment polygraph examinations are described. These standards also include, for example, the order and the context of questions used by the polygrapher during the pre-test interview or the context of various types of questions (for example, the controlled ones) used in the course of the examination (Nelson 2012; Shurany 2011). These standards are developed most often in relation to the American population. The psychophysiological bases of examinees' reactions registered during the polygraph examination are the same regardless their cultural background. On the other hand, the results of the Polish studies indicate that uncritical reliance of the expert on the interpretations of the polygraph examinations results made by algorithms of the relevant computer programs (such a possibility is given by computer programs) based on the examinations which take place in relation to the American population, can lead to making a mistake (Leśniak 2014; Leśniak and Zubańska 2010). Therefore, in our opinion, there is the need for conducting Polish empirical research in this field and modifying the American standards according to the possible intercultural differences disclosed in the Polish population. The American standards should be adapted to the Polish legal regulations, for example, in relation to the context of questions.

In the context of transparency of the polygraph examination, and the possibilities of monitoring the way of its conduct and interpreting by an expert the received configuration of psychophysiological reactions, there is the need for the use of quasi-numerical or numerical scales when interpreting the results of the examination. In Poland, many experts still makes only a qualitative assessment of the subject's reactions without specifying the particular reactions in numerical evaluations (separately in respect of each variable registered by the polygraph) while asking questions or pairs of questions (a control question – a relevant question). Such assessment is not open to any control carried out by another expert. The examination is then non-transparent. When such assessments are expressed numerically (where possible) another expert can take measurements of the examinee's reactions and verify the findings of his predecessor. Of course, the verifying expert should not know the identity of the expert who carried out the interpretation as this may be the cause of many significant errors (Dror and Charlton 2006; Dror, Charlton and Peron 2006; Kwiatkowska-Darul and Wójcikiewicz 2008).

The use of the polygraph examinations, as well as other methodologies, requires the application of an appropriate quality control system of this type of examinations. The lack of such a system results in the quality decrease of the conducted examinations. J. Konieczny (2009) amongst the methodological mistakes made by polygraphers distinguishes, amongst other things, the following ones: the experts' attachment to outdated methodologies, the use of improperly standardized methodologies or those with an unknown error area, the use of their own, often ad hoc, invented methodologies, the use of outdated methodologies imposed by the institutions who employ experts. The pre-employment polygraph examinations in state services are carried out by the experts operating within the particular service. Each service has its own experts. The lack of information flow between experts of various services (or self- isolation of experts of a particular service) allows to make methodological mistakes.

It is worth remembering that the pre-employment polygraph examinations require different standards than those used regarding the participation of the subject in a particular event. Krapohl (2002) points out that in the pre-employment examinations multiple-issue tests are usually used (the relevant questions concern a different kind of events). The relevant questions are phrased more generally than in the single-issue tests (they do not concern the participation in one event but in different events within a certain period of time). The polygraph examination is only part of a wider process of the job candidate testing (as mentioned at the beginning of this part of our chapter it is preceded by the completion of the questionnaire by the subject which usually consists of at least dozens of questions and ends with discussing the subject's reactions). An expert trained in the conduct of single-issue tests is not ergo immediately prepared to carry out the pre-employment examinations. This requires a separate training and the acquisition of the appropriate knowledge and skills.

In the practice of the pre-employment examinations a lot of methodologies are applied. In this area there are many types of the control questions tests, the tests containing only the neutral questions and relevant ones, the tests which combine (at various phases of the examination) the above mentioned tests or the tests with some other types of questions. It is important that each test which is used could fulfill the mentioned before postulates of standardization and the disclosure of the error area.

## Relevance of Pre-Employment Examinations

The relevance of the pre-employment examinations is generally lower than the relevance of the single-issue tests. However, it is not low and in the case of the best in this respect, methodologies of polygraph examinations

(Utah tests) exceeds 80% (Krapohl 2002). It is worth remembering that in the descriptive sphere there are no methods which give one hundred percent reliability of results and even in the case of DNA testing an element of subjectivity can appear in the interpretation of an expert (Dror and Hampikian 2011). In our opinion, the diagnostic value of the polygraph examinations justifies, therefore, the application of such examinations, for example, in the supervision of inmates benefiting from the probation period (Sosnowski and Wilcox 2009).

## Unification of Standards of Pre-Employment Polygraph Examinations

In the opinion of the authors of this chapter there should be the possibly unified standards for conducting the pre-employment polygraph examinations in state services. The standards should take into account the latest achievements in the field of forensic psycho physiology and set the highest professional and moral requirements for persons conducting such examinations. In particular, these standards should specify:

- The qualifications required from the persons conducting the examination together with the requirements necessary to obtain a certificate that allows to conduct the examination independently;
- The acceptable techniques and tests of conducting examinations; they should prohibit any modification ad hoc or specify the acceptable framework of such a modification;
- The way of conducting the test which precedes the polygraph examination;
- They should precisely specify the required methods of interpretation of the examination results and, at the same time, require where possible the numerical or quasi-numerical systems of interpretation of the examinations results;
- They should precisely specify the procedures of quality control of the pre-employment polygraph examinations conducted in the particular service and especially provide an annual inspection of all examinations conducted by experts in the particular service and the current control of the conducted examinations;

- The content of the subject's written statement to receive the permission for the examination;
- The elements of the examination report including the justification of the choice of the examination technique and the descriptions of the conducted tests;
- The requirement to include in the report the list of all questions asked in the particular tests;
- The rules of selection of the questions from the test that precedes the polygraph examination for this examination;
- The rules of the interview which takes place immediately after the polygraph examination;
- The way of archiving the polygraph examination (the methods of storing, also in electronic version, all the polygrams made during the examination, the way of recording verbal or non-verbal behavior of the subject that took place during the polygraph examination, during the test that preceded this examination, and also during the interview just after the examination).

Referring to the quality control of the polygraph examination, this control should be carried out, as previously mentioned, by another expert who does not know who conducted the examination before. The obstacle to such a practice can be insufficient number of polygraphers in the teams of the specific service. Perhaps the solution in such a situation would be establishing the team that would include the practitioners from several services who use the polygraph examinations. State services have their own matters covered by different kinds of confidentiality, nevertheless, we believe that to ensure the appropriate quality of the pre-employment polygraph examinations it is important to exchange information on them between the various services and to arrange the mutual management of the control of the conducted examinations.

## CONCLUSION

In our opinion, the legitimacy of the use of pre-employment polygraph examinations in the recruitment to state services leaves no doubt. The subject of the substantative discussion should be, however, different kinds of issues related to this type of examinations, for example, the importance of such an examination in the whole process or the creation of an appropriate system of the quality management. Some problems can appear while examining a particular category of people, for example, the police officers who worked undercover to conduct a surveillance of a criminal group or who, in the scope of their duties (for example, operational and reconnaissance actions), contacted with the members of the criminal group. Such individuals in the recruitment process to another service can be asked about the cooperation with the criminal group. An additional complication can be the duty of confidentiality of the circumstances of their current work.

The participation in the discussion on the use of polygraph examinations (as well as in any other) requires some basic knowledge in this field. Unfortunately, in Poland such discussions are raised by people, even academic authorities, who often do not have even basic information regarding this kind of examinations. The polygraph examination has many weaknesses which we have tried to indicate in this text. This issue should be discussed and we should try to improve the legal regulations for such examinations and the level of standardization of the examination. Apart from this, it is necessary to minimalize their error area. It is impossible to do it without reading at least part of the literature in this field. We think that there is currently no alternative to the use of such examinations for pre-employment purposes in state services (the method with sufficiently high level of standardization and known error area).

## REFERENCES

Cempura, A., Kasolik A. & Widacki, J. (2014). The current legal situation and practice the use of polygraph in Poland. In Widacki J. (Ed.) *Research Printing in Poland* (pp. 81-100). Krakow: Publishing House of the AFM.

Daniels, Ch. W. (2002) Legal aspects of polygraph admissibility in the United States. In M. Kleiner (Ed.), *Handbook of polygraph testing* (pp. 327-338). San Diego: Academic Press.

Dror, I. E. & Charlton, D. (2006). Why Experts Make Errors. *Journal of Forensic Identification*, *56* (4), pp. 600-616.

Dror, I. E., Charlton, D. & Peron, A.E. (2006). Contextual information render experts vulnerable to making erroneous identification. *Forensic Science International*, *156* (1), pp. 74-78.

Dror, I. E. & Hampikian, G. (2011). Subjectivity and bias in forensic DNA mixture interpretation. *Science & Justice*, *51* (4), pp. 204-208.

Gołaszewski, M. (2011). Report: Recent Polish Polygraph Experts Seminar – Szczytno, Poland, May 26-27, 2011. *European Polygraph, 16* (2), pp. 71-79.

Gołaszewski, M. (2013). Procedury kontroli jakości ekspertyz z zakresu badań poligraficznych. In M. Gołaszewski (Ed.), *Współczesne standardy badań poligraficznych*, (pp. 72-74). Warszawa: Agencja Bezpieczeństwa Wewnętrznego.

Herbowska, P. (2010). Research Printing worker - opportunities and threats. In Z. Goral (Ed.), *Control employee. Technical and legal dilemmas* (pp. 327-345). Warsaw: Wolters Kluwer.

Herbowska, P. & Słapczyńska, D. (2015). Printing study as a tool to support the assessment of the "small key witnesses". In E. Pływaczewski W. Filipkowski, & Z. Rau (Eds.), *Crime in the XXI century - the prevention and combating. Legal and criminological problems*, (pp. 636-652). Warsaw: Wolters Kluwer.

Konieczny, J. (2009). *Research Printing. Handbook for professionals*, Warsaw: Academic and Professional Publishing.

Konieczny, J. (2010). Polygraph examination as Scientific Evidence. *European Polygraph, 13* (3), pp. 102-157.

Kraphol, D. J. (2002). The polygraph in personnel screening. In M. Kleiner (Ed.), *Handbook of polygraph testing*, (pp. 217-236). San Diego: Academic Press.

Kwiatkowska - Darul, V. & Wójcikiewicz, J. (2008). Or "innocent need not fear"? Considerations on canvas case of Brandon Mayfield. In Kołecki H. (Ed.), *Forensic and science penalne against crime, commemorative book dedicated to Professor Miroslaw Fruit,* (pp. 334-342). Poznan: Publishing Poznan.

Lesniak, M. (2008). Ethical problems related to the expertise of the polygraph (Polygraph). In Kołecki H. (Ed.), *Forensic and science penalne against crime, commemorative book dedicated to Professor Miroslaw Fruit,* (pp. 352-366). Poznan: Publishing Poznan.

Leśniak, M. & Zubańska, M. (2010). A Comparison of Polygraph Examination Accuracy Rates Obtained Using the Seven-position Numerical Analysis Scale and the Objective Scoring System (A Study on the Polish Population). *European Polygraph, 12* (2), pp. 81-86.

Leśniak, M. (2014). Selected Problems in Evaluation of Polygraph Examination Results. *European Polygraph, 30* (4), pp. 189-196.

Memon, A., Vrij, A. & Bull, R. (2003). *Law and psychology. The credibility of the testimony and evidence,* Gdańsk: Gdańsk Publishing Psychology.

Mirska, N. (2011). Report from the 4th Interdepartmental Polygraph Seminar, Waplewo 2011. *European Polygraph, 17-18* (3-4), pp. 157-160.

Nelson, R. (2011). Directed Lie Screening – DLST. In *Normy prawne i standardy branżowe w zakresie badań poligraficznych w wybranych krajach. I Międzynarodowe Sympozjum Poligraferów. Emów, 21-24 czerwca 2010 r.* (pp. 59-72). Emów: Agencja Bezpieczeństwa Wewnętrznego.

Pasko - Porys, W. (2007). *Hearing and intelligence. Forensic Psychology*, Warsaw: Oficyna Scientific.

Shurany, T. (2011). Industry standards and legal standards in research printed in the State of Israel. In *legal standards and industry standards for research printed in the selected countries. I International Symposium Poligraferów. Jams, 21-24 June 2010.* (pp. 17-27). Jams: The Internal Security Agency.

Słapczyńska, D. (2013). Evaluation records of the tests UTAH zonal comparisons using empirical Assessment System (ESS). *Problems of Criminalistics, 282* (4), pp. 22-32.

Sosnowski D. E. & Wilcox D. T. (2009). Basics of Post-Conviction Sex Offender Polygraph Testing. In D. T. Wilcox (Ed.), *The Use of the Polygraph in Assessing, Treating and Supervising Sex Offenders: A Practitioner's Guide*, (pp. 65-95). Chichester: John Wiley & Sons Ltd.

Wiśniewski, L. (2005). Polygraph Tests in the Border Guard. In J. Bryk, A. Szajowska, & M. Zubańska (Eds.), *Research Polygraph in Polish criminal law* (pp. 23-26). Szczytno: Publisher of the Police Academy.

Wójcikiewicz, J. (2004). Research Printing (Polygraph) employee and officer. In A. Bulsiewicz, A. Marcus, & V. Kwiatkowska - Darul (Eds.), *Doctrine Multiplex Veritas Una Book of Jubilee offered Professor Mariusz Kulickiemu*, (pp. 31-40). Torun: Nicolaus Copernicus University Press.

Zubańska, M. (2010), Research psychophysiological police officers. In Z. Goral (Ed.), *Control employee. Technical and legal dilemmas*, (pp. 321-326). Warsaw: Wolters Kluwer.

In: Law Enforcement and Crime
Editor: Emanuel T. Rhodes
ISBN: 978-1-63484-127-6


*Chapter 2*

# FORENSIC ENTOMOLOGY: INSECTS AS EVIDENCE: A POTENTIAL TOOL AS A FORENSIC INDICATOR IN THE LAW ENFORCEMENT TECHNOLOGY

***Kaliyaperumal Karunamoorthi****
Unit of Tropical Diseases, Department of Environmental Health, Faculty of Public Health and Tropical Medicine, Jazan University, Jazan, Kingdom of Saudi Arabia

## ABSTRACT

In recent years, criminal justice system necessitates the coordination of multidisciplinary professionals such as investigators, magistrates and scientists. Forensic entomology is in practice ever since the thirteenth century, and remains as one of the key scientific tools ensuring precision for medico-legal and criminal investigations. It includes the collection, documentation, preservation and analysis of insects and other arthropods as evidences in the legal context. It is mainly employed to determine the elapsed time since death [Postmortem interval; (PMI)] in case of suspicious death, e.g., homicide and suicide investigations by inferring with various both abiotic and biotic parameters like entomological evidence, geoclimaticdata, location and condition of the corpse, etc.

* E-mail:karunamoorthi@gmail.com. Mobile:+ 966-504-192-938; Fax:+ 966-17321-0579.

Indeed cadaverous critters provide decisive clues about a crime by estimating the age of the oldest necrophagous insects that developed on the corpse, or by analyzing the insect species composition on the corpse. Two major groups of insect's viz., Dipterans (True flies/Mosquitoes/ Gnats/Midges) and Coleopterans (beetles) are primarily used as forensic indicators. Carrion entomofauna analysis as a forensic tool has acquired more recognition as the blow flies (*Diptera: Calliphoridae*) and flesh flies (*Diptera: Sarchophagidae*) are the first creatures to locate and colonize the cadavers within ten-minutes of demise. Interestingly, they are capable of sensing corpse from as far as ten-miles away. Many insect species are engaged at each stage of carcass decomposition. Arthropod succession patterns and developmental rates of succession entomofauna enable effective investigation, if the murderee has been dead for a month or longer.

Entomological evidences are often more accurate and sometimes the only scientifically reliable forensic technique of estimating PMI, which subsequently could lead to death probe. It is equally helpful in determining the circumstances of abuses and sexual-molestation too. Besides, it is extremely useful in various steps of investigation like; (1) estimating the time of death, (2) movement of the corpse, (3) manner and cause of demise, (4) create a link between perpetrator and suspect with the death scene, and (5) detection of toxins, drugs, or even the DNA of the victim through molecular analysis of insect samples. It often validates the identity of a victim too. However, the significance of forensic entomology is often undermined or overlooked in the emerging economies due to lack of resources and skilled professionals. Therefore, adequate forensic entomology laboratory facilities must be set up in each province as there is a great need for research in order to assist the criminal justice system in the near future.

**Keywords:** forensic entomology, law enforcement, crime investigation, forensic indicators

## INTRODUCTION

Insects belong to the phylum called 'arthropoda' and their body is divided into three segments viz. head, thorax and abdomen with three pair [hexapoda; (six legs)] of jointed legs, a pair of compound eye and antennae. The genome sequencing data analysis reveal that the insects might have evolved nearly 480 million years ago during the Ordovician Era [1]; comparatively whereas human have existed merely about three-million years ago [2]. The oldest insect fossil, '*Rhyniognathahirsti*' is estimated to be about 407 to 396 million years archaic [1]. The most diverse insect groups appear to have coevolved with flowering plants.

At the moment, there are nearly 700,000 insects species have been described. However, still more than ten-million species yet to be identified. Insects potentially represent over ninety percent of animals [3]. In the history of earth, global climatic conditions have changed several times, which have apparently altered the diversity of insects. Currently they are one of the most diversified taxonomic groups on the planet. They have adopted and dominated in a wide-range of climatic zones and ecosystem [3]. Insects are serving as a key investigative and criminalistics tool to probe homicide, suicide, untimely death, and other violent crimes.

Forensic entomology is 'the use of the insects, and their arthropod relatives that inhabit decomposing remains to aid legal investigations' [4]. American Board of Forensic Entomology (1997) [5] defined it as 'it's using insect evidence to uncover circumstances of interest to the law'. It is a subset of the forensic sciences whereby information and samples of insects and associated arthropods are gathered and analysed to help draw conclusions on legal matters from a crime scene [2]. It is categorized into three-sub-fields: (1) urban, (2) stored products, and (3) medico-criminal forensic entomology.

Data obtained by forensic entomological investigation can be employed to pinpoint the place of death as well as to estimate the post-mortem interval (PMI). Globally, it is extremely helpful to solve the events surrounding felonies or serious crimes, particularly violent delinquencies like rape, suicide, murder and several other aspects of crime, such as physical abuse and contraband trafficking [6, 7]. Besides, though forensic entomology is now commonly used to determine the time of death, it can be equally applicable to resolve wildlife crimes too. In animal cases, many species have a legal hunting season, meaning that animals killed outside this time are poached. In such cases, if the time of death was known it would conclusively indicate whether an animal was killed legally or illegally out of season [8].

In the medico-legal investigation, it is important to understand whether drugs, toxins and/or alcohol consumption occurred prior to death [9, 10]. Consequently, now medico-legal forensic entomology is also helpful in the relatively new field of entomotoxicology. It involves the utilization of entomological specimens as toxicological indicators to detect ante- or perimortem ingestion of drugs, toxins or alcohol that may have possibly caused the death of the victim [11] as these factors can sometimes contribute to reconstruct the crime scene as well as to point out the possible manner of death.

Traditionally, tissue, blood, or urine samples are often analysed for the existence of the toxic and other harmful substances in the cadavers. However, in many drug or alcohol related deaths, the decedents are often undetectable in an advanced stage of carcass decomposition [11]. Furthermore, it is important to note that the traditional human samples are unobtainable during this stage. In this context, anthropophagic insects could provide alternate toxicological specimens for analysis [12]. Because these insects are usually subsist in putrefying remains and serve as a worthy alternative sample to identify the drugs and toxins present in the decomposing tissue [12].

In the past decades, several researchers have emphasized the essentialities of entomotoxicology in the detection of toxic and controlled substances through arthropod-analyses [13-15] including different drugs. Drugs within a corpse may affect the development rate of insects [16] that feed on them. For examples drugs and poisons like Morphine [17], heroin [18], Opiates [19, 20], cocaine [13], barbiturates [21], clomipramine, amitryptiline [18], nortriptyline, levomepromezine and tioridazine [22, 23], Diazepam [24], hydrocortisone, Sodium methohexital [25], Methadone [26], methamphetamine [15], phencyclidine [27] and Malathion [28] are commonly involved in cases where forensic entomology is used.

At the moment, indeed forensic entomology has attracted global attention, particularly among the investigators, forensic experts, coroners, medical examiners, and pathologists. Forensic entomologists primarily focus on the criminal investigation by dealing with the necrophagous insects. Perhaps, they can play a pivotal role in cases of badly decomposed and unidentified remains and with an undetermined time of death [29]. Adequate knowledge on distribution of arthropods in the particular locality and how they react to various bio-geo-climatic factors considerably improves the estimation of PMI as well as in determining whether the carcass was relocated from another location/region too [30]. In recent years, artifacts produced by arthropods and the proof of neglect of elderly persons and children have become a special focus of interest in forensic entomology [31].

In the past decade, the general acceptance of arthropods as forensic indicators has progressively increased worldwide. Scientific analysis and expert opinion of qualified forensic entomologists are now routinely solicited by law enforcement and legal professionals for both criminal and civil investigations globally, particularly in the industrialized economies. This widespread acceptance of forensic entomology within the criminal justice system has created a high demand for entomological services [30]. International scientific institutions have already established several specific forensic entomology laboratories to assist the law enforcement agencies to probe death cases [32].

Insects are major players in the nature's recycling process. Nature rapidly populates a corpse with a diverse community of organisms, particularly insects to reduce the body in to its basic components [33]. Forensic scientists can estimate the PMI, any changes in position of the corpse as well as the cause of death by studying the corpse fauna [34]. Perhaps, forensic entomologists play a pivotal role in crime scene analysis by means of assisting the various criminal investigation professionals along with law enforcement authorities to reconstruct the events. Eventually he/she must testify in the court prosecution to expound insect-related evidence found at crime scenes and corpses.

In these perspectives, this chapter becomes more significant and pertains. It shall provide a detailed outline on the crucial role of forensic entomologists in the criminal investigation by using insects as forensic indicators/evidence in the law enforcement technology. In addition, it shall also elaborate the history, commonly used forensic insects, various stages of carcass decomposition process, and various scientific methodologies adopted in investigation like interpreting the relationship between insect type and the stages of death in detail.

## HISTORY OF FORENSIC ENTOMOLOGY

Forensic entomology is not a new discipline and the history dates back to the thirteen-century. Song Ci [or Sung Tz'u; (1186-1249)] an outstanding forensic scientist in the Southern Song Dynasty of China, had documented the first forensic entomology criminal-case in his book 'XiyuanJilu' (Collected Writings on the 'Washing Away of Wrongs'). This is the first as well as earliest monographic work on forensic medicine in the world and it was written in 1247 [35]. In his judicial examination/investigation, he identified the murderer through forensic flies which flew to the sickle, which had been used in committing the crime. This sickle had bits of soft tissue, blood, bone and hair attached to it and thus attracted the flies. Then confessed himself the perpetrator of the deed and 'knocked his head on the floor' [36, 37].

However, the first application of forensic entomology in a modern court house was in eighteenth-century in France, where entomological data was admitted as proof for acquitting the current occupants of the residence from where the skeletonized remains of a child were found [38] Megnin (1894) [39] was one of the earliest researchers, who has observed that different insect species arrive at and lay eggs on a corpse at very specific times of decomposition process. In the United Kingdom, blowfly larvae are featured in the first successful usage of entomological evidence, when they were discovered on decaying human remains dumped in a small ravine in Dumfriesshire, Scotland, in September 1935. Subsequently, the remains were identified as those of the wife and maid of Dr Buck Ruxton (Lancaster). The maggots were aged by Dr A. G. Mearns (forensic entomologist) and provided vital evidence as to when the murders took place. Dr Ruxton was consequently convicted of the murders and hanged [39].

In the United States of America, an event reported by Haskell et al. (1996) [40] shows the valuable use of entomological evidence during a murder investigation, where a corpse of a man was found beside his resident. The last time the victim had been seen, he and his wife were engaged in a bitter argument. The wife claimed that she had last seen her husband two days ago, while the forensic entomologist refused the wife's alibi as the maggots noted on the corpse when located were oldest than two days. Subsequently, the wife was charged with first-degree murder. In the past decade, forensic entomology has become more and more common in police investigations. Therefore, insect specimens, such as blowfly larvae (maggots) or adults, must be considered as other physical evidences like blood stains, fingerprints, hairs, fibres, or any other biological materials [41]. Consequently, forensic flies should be processed and identified as evidence at the crime scene examination as well as at autopsy too [42, 43]. By considering the importance of forensic entomology, in 1996, the American Board of Forensic Entomology has been developed certification Board for Forensic Entomologists, similar to the Board certification available for forensic odontologists and forensic anthropologists.

## IMPORTANCE OF FORENSIC ENTOMOLOGY

In the classical forensic methods, the pathologists estimate the time of death based on various biological parameters, like lividity, rigor mortis, postmortem cooling, changes in the chemical constituents of body, autolysis of tissue, and the decomposition as a result of bacterial activity in the body. However, these parameters are not reliable beyond about seventy-two hours after death [44]. In this context, the existing forensic-entomological method of determining PMI was found to be statistically more reliable and accurate when compared with other conventional pathological methods, particularly during the later stages of decay [45]. It is interesting to note that insect life cycles act as precise clocks which begin within minutes of death. They can also reveal that whether the dead-body has been relocated after death too [46].

## EXISTING METHOD TO DETERMINE ELAPSED TIME-SINCE-DEATH

The primary purpose of forensic entomology today is to determine elapsed time-since-death. There are two main ways of using insects to determine PMI and the method used is determined by the circumstances of each and every case [47];

1. *Maggot age and development method* is mainly used when death occurred less than a month prior to finding. The degree of development of the oldest maggots (larvae of Dipteran flies) feeding on the corpse indicates a close approximation to time-since-death, as insects typically start oviposition within minutes or hours of death [36].
2. *Successional wave of insects' method* is used when the corpse has been dead for between a month up to a year or more. Since insects arrive at decomposing remains in predictable, successive waves based on the stage of decomposition [48, 49].

### 1. Maggot Age and Development Method

It can provide accurate information about the date of death, or a range of days, and is mainly used in the first few weeks of after death. Blowflies are mainly employed here, since they are highly attracted towards a corpse and arrive instantly after death (Table 1). They lay their eggs on the corpse, usually in a wound, if present, otherwise in any of the natural orifices. The egg is laid in batches then hatches, into a first instar (stage) larva (maggot). Subsequently the larva continuously feed on the corpse and moults into second, successively third instar larva. Finally the third instar, wanders away from the corpse, either into the clothes or the soil, to pupate [47]. The immature stage varies from the adults in terms of structure, habit, and habitat. After a number of days, an adult fly will emerge from the pupa and the cycle will continue again (Figure 1).

Duration of lifecycle is mainly governed by the availability of food and the climatic conditions in a particular location.

An analysis of the oldest stage of the insect on the corpse and the temperature of the region in which the body was found leads to a day or range of days in which the first insects oviposited or laid eggs on the corpse. For example, if the oldest insects are seven-days old, then the decedent has been killed for at least seven days. This method is extremely helpful until the first adults begin to emerge, afterwards it is quite impossible to determine which generation of maggots is existing. However, after a single blowfly generation, the time of death can be well-established by using another technique called the 'insect succession method' [47].

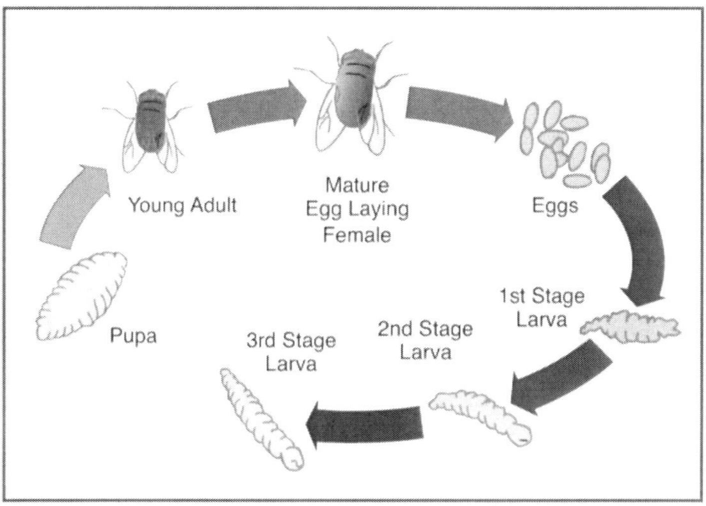


Figure 1. The life cycle of fly.

## 2. Successional Waves of Insects' Method

Insects arrive on a cadaver in a predictable sequence depending on the stages of decomposition. This is termed as insect succession or faunal succession. Forensic entomologists study this process to assist medico-legal investigations. Human body, or any kind of carrion, changes very rapidly depending on the ecosystem of a particular geographic region from the fresh state to dry bones in a matter of weeks or months. During the decomposition process, the remains undergo rapid physical, biological and chemical vicissitudes. The insects do not visit carrion at the same time, but in sequential 'waves'; each stage of decomposition is attractive to different group of sarcosaprophagous insects [47]. If the forensic entomologist can determine the sequence of colonizing insects, it can be analysed to estimate the time of death [50].

Certain insects' species are often the key witnesses to a crime and they usually arrive within 24 hour of death if the season is suitable i.e., spring, summer or fall in Canada and can arrive within minutes in the presence of blood or other body fluids. Some insects are attracted directly by the carrion, which is used as a food source or an oviposition medium, whereas a few other species are attracted by the large aggregation of other insects, which provide them a food resource [51]. Among flies, there are three waves of colonisation of a body;(1) the primary wave - the arrival of blow flies, (2) the secondary wave - the arrival of the flesh flies (Table 1) and (3) the tertiary wave - arrival of Black Carrion Fly (*Hydrotaea rostrata*), among others in Western Australia [50]. Several species are not interested in the corpse when the body is fresh, but they may be attracted to the corpse in later decomposing stages like cheese skippers, which arrive later, during the protein fermentation stage [51].

**Table 1. Typical faunal succession pattern (Source: Smith 1986) [52]**

| Succession wave | Principle insect fauna | State of corpse | Age of corpse |
|---|---|---|---|
| 1 | Blow flies | Fresh | First 3 months |
| 2 | Blow flies and flesh flies | Odour | First 3 months |
| 3 | Dermestid beetles | Fats are rancid | 3-6 months |
| 4 | Various flies | Fats are rancid | 3-6 months |
| 5 | Various flies and beetles | Ammonia fermentation | 4-8 months |
| 6 | Mites | Ammonia fermentation | 6-12 months |
| 7 | Dermestid beetles | Completely dried | 1-3 years |
| 8 | Beetles | Completely dried | 3 + years |

Numerous insects' species are involved at each decomposition stage. Therefore, with knowledge of the regional insect fauna and times of carrion colonization, the insect assemblage associated with the remains can be analyzed to determine a window of time in which death/crime took place. This method is used when the decedent has been dead from a few weeks up to a year, or in some cases several years after death, with the estimated window of time broadening as time since death increases. It can also be helpful to indicate the season of death [47]. Various environmental factors considerably affect the insects' succession pattern. These includes: season, sun-light exposure, whether the body was found indoor, immersed in water or in urban vs rural area. Bodies that are buried, left in vehicles, found in enclosed spaces, hanged or burnt are also subject to varying insect succession patterns.

## The Process of Decay of the Corpse

The process of decay begins at the moment of death. Initially cells start dying and autolysis occurs, ultimately the body begins decomposing. The gastrointestinal tract bacteria also start to destroy the soft tissue and produce various liquids and gases like hydrogen sulphide, carbon dioxide, methane, ammonia, sulfur dioxide and hydrogen. The decomposing corpse releases the volatile molecules called 'apeneumones,' which is responsible to attract insects immediately [34]. Crag et al. (1950) [53] identified that putrative sulfur-based compounds were also responsible for the initial attract of flies, however oviposition are mainly induced by ammonium-rich compounds [53]. Several researchers isolated various volatile chemicals released at different stages of decomposition. These volatile molecules significantly alter the insect behavior according to the specific stages of decomposition [54].

The corpse decomposition process can be classified into five stages on the basis of physical appearance, internal temperatures and characteristic of insect populations [55, 56];

1. *Fresh stage (Days 1-2)*: The body looks relatively normal. Blow and flesh flies arrive within ten-minutes of death [55]. Cellular breakdown occurs without any morphological alterations. Though morphological changes and odors are not recognizable to humans, the released chemicals attract insects (LeBlanc and Logan 2010). Subsequently blow flies lay their eggs, which quickly hatch into maggots and begin to feed on the corpse tissues. However, flesh flies do not lay eggs, but deposit newly hatched maggots. [55],
2. *Bloated stage (Days 2-7)*: The gases generated by the metabolic activities of anaerobic bacteria cause an inflation of the abdomen and forming a balloon-like appearance. Arthropod activities combined with the putrefaction processes raise the internal temperatures of the corpse. The greatest numbers of adult *Diptera* were attracted. First-

and early second-instar larval stages were present by the fourth-day [34]. Subsequently, house flies and the other flies maggots form feeding masses that help to liquefy the tissues [56].

3. *Decay stage (Days 5-13)*: The skin breaks and gases escape, provide a deflated look. The maggot masses are large and very active and that smells bad [56]. The internal temperature rises to $14^{0}$C above the ambient temperature followed by a drop of signifying the end of the decay stage [34]. Most of the maggots complete their development and start to leave the corpse in order to pupate under the soil. Most of the flesh is broken from the corpse, except cartilage, bone, and skin remaining [56].
4. *Post-decay stage (Days 10-23):* It begins when most of the *Diptera larvae* leave the carcass, leaving behind bones, cartilage, hair, small portions of tissue, and a large amount of wet, viscous material known as byproducts of decay (BOD). The BOD is the primary site of arthropod activity during this stage [34].
5. *Remains stage (Days 18-90 +)*: It is characterized by bones with little cartilage remaining and the BOD has dried up [34]. The transition from post-decay to remain stage is gradual, with declining adult and larval *Diptera* populations [55].

## Common Forensic Flies Used in the Medico-Legal Investigation

More than sixty-insect families play a pivotal role in carrion ecology [52]. However, only the families (*Calliphoridae*, *Sarcophagidae* and *Muscidae*) of *Diptera* (Flies) (Figure 2) and the families (*Silphidae, Staphylinidae, Cleridae* and *Dermestidae*) of Coleoptera (beetles) are the most important in the forensic entomology (Table 2) [57, 58]. These insects are found worldwide, making them as a useful forensic indicator by providing valuable clues and evidence in death and criminal cases in forensic investigations [59]. The following major insects (flies and beetles) are extremely helpful to resolve the criminal cases (Table 2). Particularly, the skipper fly *(Piophila nigriceps)*, is found only in urban settings [56].

| | |
|---|---|
| 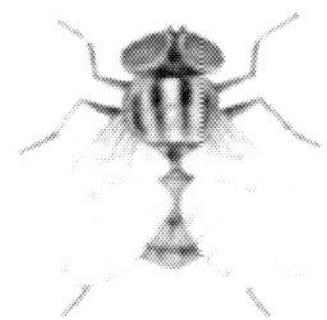 | 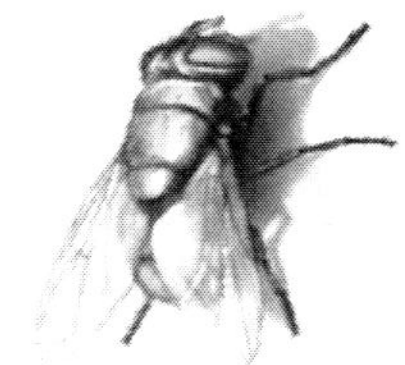 |
| **House Fly** (*Muscidae*) | **Blow Fly** (*Calliphoridae*) |
|  | 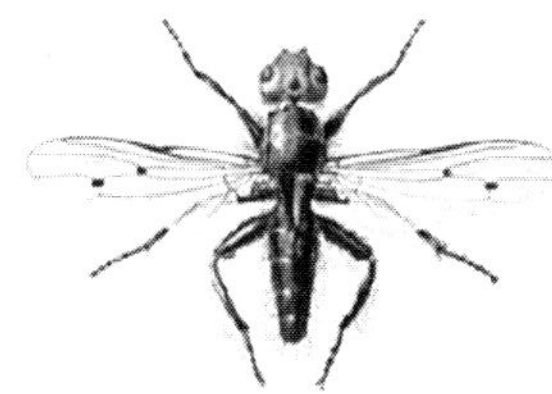 |
| **Flesh Fly** (*Sarcophagidae*) | **Skipper Fly** (*Piophilidae*) |

Figure 2. Four common forensic flies.

**Table 2. Major Necrophagous Dipteran Flies and Coleopteran Beetles very commonly employed in forensic entomology investigations**

| S. No. | Dipteran Flies | | Coleopteran Beetles | |
|---|---|---|---|---|
| | Family | Common name(s) | Family | Common name(s) |
| 1 | *Calliphoridae* | Blow Flies | *Silphidae* | Carrion Beetles |
| 2 | *Sarchophagidae* | Flesh Flies | *Dermestidae* | Skin Beetles, Leather Beetles, Hide Beetles, Carpet Beetles and Larder Beetles |
| 3 | *Muscidae* | Muscid Flies | *Staphylinidae* | Rove Beetles |
| 4 | *Piophilidae* | Skipper Flies | *Histeridae* | Clown Beetles |
| 5 | *Scathophagidae* | Dung Flies | *Cleridae* | Checkered Beetles |
| 6 | *Sepsidae* | Black Scavenger Flies | *Trogidae* | Hide Beetles |
| 7 | *Sphaeroceridae* | Small Dung Flies and Minute Dung Flies | *Scarabaeidae* | Scarab Beetles |
| 8 | *Stratiomyidae* | Soldier Flies | *Nitidulidae* | Sap Beetles |
| 9 | *Phoridae* | Humpbacked Flies or Scuttle Flies | - | - |
| 10 | *Psychodidae* | Moth Flies, Sand Flies and Owl Midges | - | - |

## Other Insects

- *Moths* - During the final phases of decomposition, certain species of moth may visit the remains to feed upon the hair of the deceased.
- *Mites* - mites have been known to frequent the scene of a decomposing body at numerous stages in the decay process, with some feeding on the corpse shortly after death and others devouring the dry skin in later stages of decomposition. They can be found on the body itself or in the soil underneath the remains.
- *Bees, Wasps, Ants and Spiders* - Other insects like certain bees, wasps, ants and spiders are not attracted to the decomposing remains, but still visit the death scene to prey upon other insects.

## Collection and Preservation of Insects Specimens

Taxonomic identification of the insects found on corpses is extremely crucial to the reconstruction of events surrounding criminal cases involving death. The time of death, can usually be determined by using insect evidence gathered from in and around of a corpse, if the evidence is properly collected, preserved and analyzed by an appropriately experienced forensic entomologist (Figure 3) [46]. A core element to the utilization of arthropods as forensic indicators is the proper identification, documentation, collection, and shipment of entomological evidence from human or animal remains [30].

Proper collection procedures dictate collections of live and preserved samples at the scene, following which autopsy will be performed. In addition to the actual collection of arthropods, the investigator must thoroughly document the circumstances of the death, like all insect activity, create evidence labels for all collected entomological samples, and document environmental habitats at the scene as well as current geoclimatic data [50].

The judicial system mandates the utilization of best practices and proceedings that ensure that proper custody is maintained. Thus, a proper chain of custody should be established for entomological evidence as soon as it is collected. Entomological documentation and collection at the scene can be broken down into several major steps as shown in the Figure 4 [30]. Once the

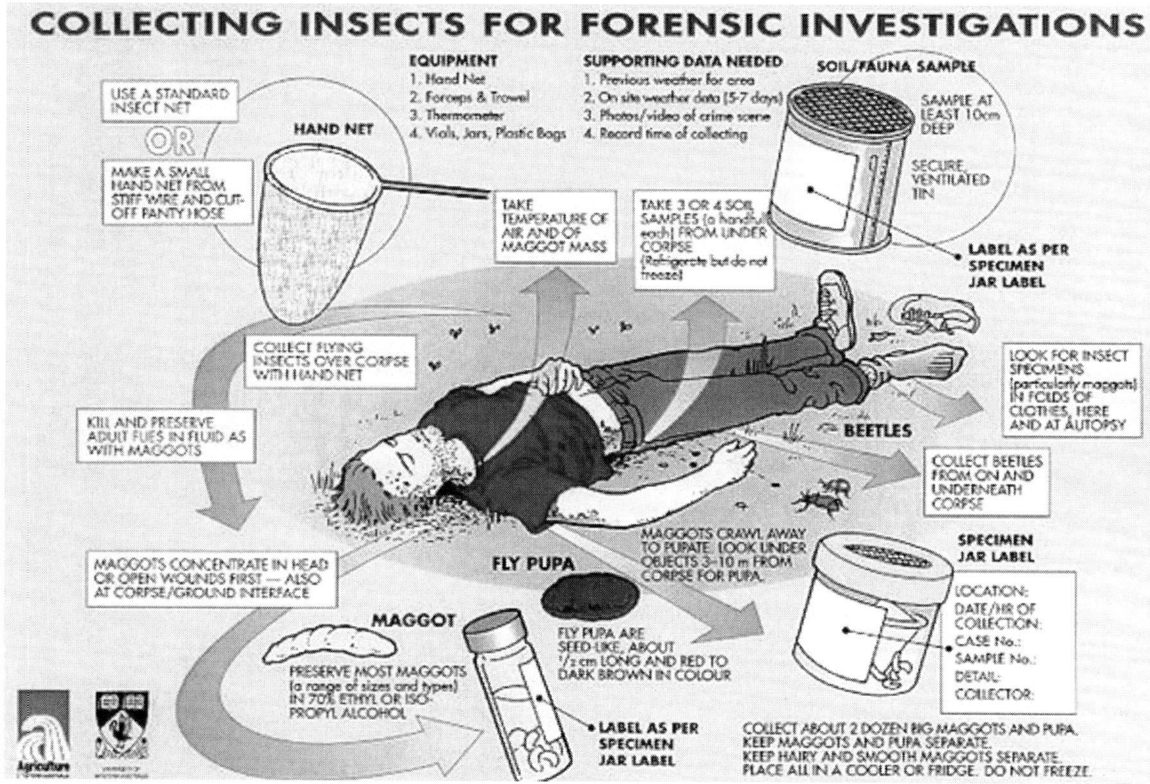


Figure 3. Collection of insects for forensic investigation (Source: Byrd et al., 2010) [30].

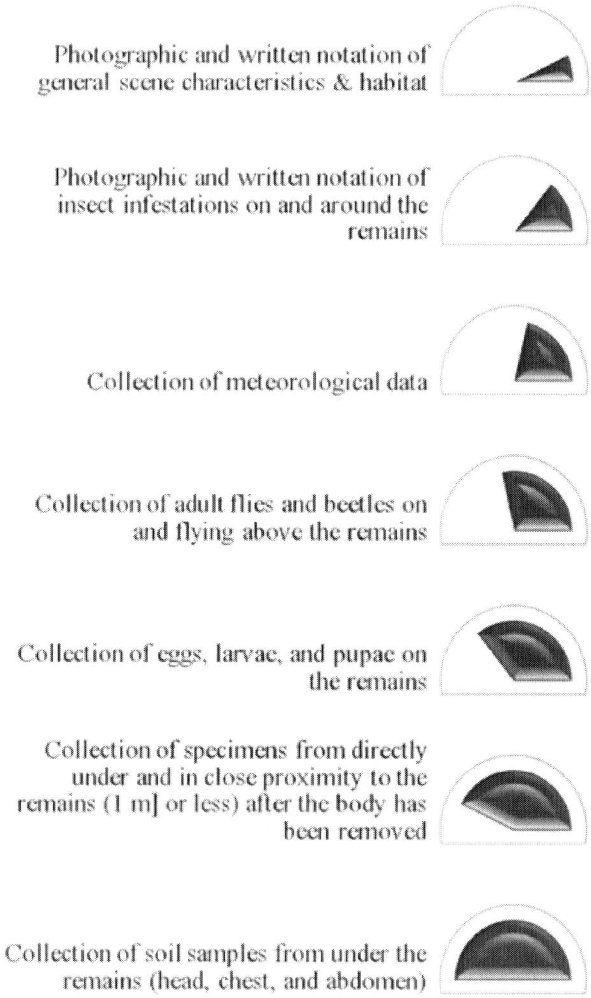


Figure 4. Major steps involved in the documentation and collection of the entomological specimens in a typical crime scene.

species of fly has been collected and identified, the forensic entomologist will develop a lifecycle model of the fly. The models can be developed from the previous criminal investigations or controlled laboratory experiments. Lifecycles of flies are variable between species and depending on environmental conditions too [50].

## Steps in Estimating the Post-Mortem Index (PMI)

The estimation of time of death by entomological data after 24 h is more accurate than medical examiner's estimation through soft tissue examination [55] and sometimes the only method to determine the elapsed time since death [60]. Besides, up to one month the PMI can be assessed through insect larvae present on the carcass [61]. Blowflies are the first creatures that reach cadaver and the females lay eggs within hours after death and begin its lifecycle (Figure 2).

The forensic entomologist estimates how long it takes to reach each different stages (larva, pupa and preadult/imago) in an insect's lifecycle. Subsequently he/she calculate the time since the egg was laid and the age of the insects is extremely helpful to estimate PMI [62, 63]. It is important to note that though the age of insect is correct, the death of the victim usually occurred prior to the oviposition. This period is quite variable and highly depends on temperature and time of day the death occurred. Besides, the key-factors like whether the corpse is exposed or buried in soil or immersed in water also must be considered [62, 63]. Furthermore, insects are also helpful to establish whether the corpse has been moved after death, by linking local fauna around the body, and the fauna on the carcass [62, 63].

The rate of development of the larvae is highly associated with surrounding ambient temperatures and once the thermal history of the larvae is obtained, it can be compared with temperatures at the death scene and eventually the PMI can be projected. The successional patterns of carrion arthropods could also be useful to assess the PMI, as insects arrive at a corpse in a predictable specific manner in a particular location and environmental conditions [48, 64, 65]. Nevertheless, whenever insect development data are unobtainable, the time of death can be predictable by using succession data. In such cases, the PMI is assessed by comparing corpse fauna with the composition of arthropod-assemblage at a given period of time derived from an animal model (baseline fauna) [66].

## Impact of Bio-Geo-Climatic Factors on the Insects' Lifecycle

Indeed, temperature is one of the key external factors, which is strongly correlated with the metabolic activity of 'cold-blooded' insect's maggots.

They develop more rapidly at higher temperatures and slower at lower-temperatures. The size can also be significantly pretentious by quantity and availability of food resources as well as by the numbers of competing maggots. Toxic substances in or on a corpse can be accumulated by feeding larvae, which notably interrupts the rate of development. Addictive stimulants like cocaine and heroin significantly boost the development-rate of larvae, thereby affecting the accuracy of PMI estimates if not taken into consideration [38]. Each forensic case is unique due to the involvement of higher number of variables and this can make it extremely difficult to assess often scanty data with great accuracy.

## A Need for Further Research

Though currently much is well-known on the life-cycle of the blowfly, there is considerable scope for future morphological, biochemical and molecular research to improve our identification skills as well as precise estimation of PMI. It includes details of the influence of corpse location and covering on fly access, the impact of diurnal cycles and of temperatures on fly and maggot activity, and ways in which the metabolic activity of a mass of maggots raises temperatures and affects their development. Scanning electron microscopy is increasingly being used for routine identification and will be of considerable value in the future, especially for the identification of eggs and larvae. Besides, further research will enhance forensic entomology as a genuine, quantitative scientific discipline, and improve the quality and accuracy of the case reconstructions and the accurate estimation of PMI [38].

Globally, several researchers have demonstrated that forensic entomology is a valuable adjunct to death investigations through various case-studies [67-70]. However, our knowledge on the biology and ecology of fauna associated with the decomposing corpse must be well-refined. Catts (1992) [71] has extensively discussed the shortfalls and issues related in order to estimate the PMI, a key element in any death investigation. Therefore, immediate further fields as well as laboratory-based experimental researches are warranted. They should be expanded to include buried, emersed, burned or enclosed carrion. The array of other invertebrates associated with corpse decomposition is extensive and complex, and much more knowledge of them is also required [71].

## ACKNOWLEDGMENTS

The authors would like to acknowledge Ms. L. Melita for her sincere assistance in editing the manuscript. Our last but not least heartfelt thanks go to our colleagues from the Department of Environmental Health, Faculty of Public Health and Tropical Medicine, Jazan University, Kingdom of Saudi Arabia, for their kind support and cooperation.


## REFERENCES


[1] Michael, E. S., Grimaldi, D. A. New light shed on the oldest insect. *Nature*, 2004; 427(6975):627-630.

[2] Magni, P., Guercini, S., Leighton, A., Dadour, I. Forensic entomologists: An evaluation of their status. *Journal of Insect Science*, 2013; 13:78.

[3] Erwin, T. L. Tropical forests: their richness in Coleoptera and other arthropod species. *Coleopt. Bulletin*, 1982; 36:74-75.

[4] Byrd, J. H., Castner, J. L. *Forensic Entomology: The Utility of Arthropods in Legal Investigations*. CRC Press, Florida. 1st ed. 2000; 1-225.

[5] American Board of Forensic Entomology. *Welcome to the World of Forensic Entomology*. [Internet] Available at: World Wide Web, http:// www.missouri.edu/cafnr/entomology/index.html. 1997.

[6] eh, B. Scope and Applications of Forensic Entomology. *Ann. Rev. Entomol.* 1985; 30:137-154.

[7] Catts, E. P., Goff, M. L. Forensic entomology in criminal investigations. *Annu Rev Entomol.* 1992; 37:253-72.

[8] Anderson, G. S. Wildlife forensic entomology: determining time of death in two illegally killed black bear cubs. *J Forensic Sci* 1999; 44(4): 856-859.

[9] Miller, M. L., Lord, W. D., Goff, M. L. Donnelly, B; McDonough, E. T., Alexis, J. C. Isolation of Amitriptyline and Nortriptyline from fly *puparia* (*Phoridae*) and beetle *exuviae* (*Dermestidae*) associated with mummified human remains. *Journal of Forensic Sciences*, 1994; 39: 1305-1313.

[10] Beyer, J. C., Enos, W. F., Stajic, M. Drug identification through analyses of maggots. *Journal of Forensic Sciences*, 1980; 25:411-412.

[11] Goff, M. L., Lord, W. D. *Entomotoxicology*. In, Forensic Entomology: The Utility of Arthropods in Legal Investigations. Byrd, J. H. and Castner, J. L., Eds. CRC Press, Boca Raton. 2010.

[12] Tabor, K. L. *Succession and Development Studies on Carrion Insects of Forensic Importance*. Dissertation submitted to the Faculty of Virginia Polytechnic Institute and State University in partial fulfillment of the requirements for the degree of Doctor of Philosophy in Entomology. 10th May 2004.

[13] Goff, M. L., Omori, A. I., Goodbrod, J. R. Effect of cocaine in tissues on the development rate of Boettcheriscaperegrina (*Diptera: Sarcophagidae*). *J Med Entomol*, 1989; 26:91-93.

[14] Goff, M. L., Brown, W. A., Hewadikaram, K. A., Omori, A. I. Effect of heroin in decomposing tissues on the development rate of Boettcherisca peregrine (*Diptera: Sarcophagidae*) and implications of this effect on estimation of postmortem intervals using arthropod development patterns. *J Forensic Sci*. 1991; 36:537-542.

[15] Goff, M. L., Brown, W. A., Omori, A. I. Preliminary observations of the effect of methamphetamine in decomposing tissues on the development rate of *Parasarcophaga ruficornis* (*Diptera: Sarcophagidae*) and implications of this effect on the estimations of postmortem intervals. *J Forensic Sci*. 1992; 37:867-872.

[16] O'Brien, C., Turner, B. Impact of paracetamol on *Calliphora vicina* larval development. *Int J Legal Med*. 2004; 118:188-189.

[17] Hédouin, V., Bourel, B., Bécart, A., Tournel, G., Deveaux, M. et al. Determination of drug levels in larvae of *Protophormia terraenovae* and *Calliphora vicina* (*Diptera: Calliphoridae*) reared on rabbit carcasses containing morphine. *J. Forensic Sci*. 2001; 46:12-14.

[18] Goff, M. L., Brown, W. A., Omori, A. I., Lapointe, D. A. Preliminary observations of the effects of amitriptyline in decomposing tissues on the development of *Parasarcophaga ruficornis* (*Diptera: Sarcophagidae*) and implications of this effect to estimation of postmortem interval. *J Forensic Sci*. 1993; 38:316-322.

[19] Bourel, B., Fleurisse, L., Hedouin, V., Cailliez, J. C., Creusy, C. et al. Immunohistochemical contribution to the study of morphine metabolism in *Calliphoridae larvae* and implications in forensic Entomotoxicology. *J Forensic Sci*. 2001; 46:596-599.

[20] Bourel, B., Tournel, G., Hedouin, V., Deveaux, M., Goff, M. L. et al. Morphine extraction in necrophagous insects remains for determining ante-mortem opiate intoxication. *Forensic Sci Int*. 2001; 120:127-131.

[21] Tracqui, A., Keyser-Tracqui, C., Kintz, P., Ludes, B. Entomotoxicology for the forensic toxicologist: much ado about nothing? *Int J Legal Med* 2004; 118:194-196.

[22] Campobasso, C. P., Disney, R. H. L., Introna, F. A. Case of *Megaselia scalaris* (*Diptera: Phoridae*) Breeding in Human Corpse. *Aggarwal's Internet Journal of Forensic Medicine and Toxicology* 2004; 5:3-5.

[23] Campobasso, C. P., Gherardi, M., Caligara, M., Sironi, L. et al. Drug analysis in blowfly larvae and in human tissues: a comparative study. *Int J Legal Med* 2004; 118: 210-214.

[24] Carvalho, L. M. L., Thyssen, P. J., Goff, M. L., Linhares, A. X. Observations on the Succession Patterns of Necrophagous Insects on a Pig Carcass in an Urban Area of South Eastern Brazil. *Aggarwal's Internet Journal of Forensic Medicine and Toxicology* 2004; 5:33-39.

[25] Musvasva, E., Williams, K. A., Muller, W. J., Villet, M. H. Preliminary observations on the effects of hydrocortisone and sodium methohexital on development of *Sarcophaga (Curranea) tibialis* Mac quart (*Diptera*: *Sarcophagidae*), and implications for estimating post mortem interval. *Forensic Sci Int*. 2001; 120:37-41.

[26] Behonick, G. S., Massello, W., Kuhlman, J. J. Jr., Saady, J. A tale of two drugs in Southwestern Virginia: oxycodone and methadone. *Proceedings American Academy of Forensic Sciences*, 20: 312-313, Chicago, IL., February 2003.

[27] Goff, M. L., Brown, W. A., Omori, A. I., Lapointe, D. A. Preliminary observations of the effects of phencyclidine in decomposing tissues on the development of *Parasarcophaga ruficornis* (*Diptera*: *Sarcophagidae*). *J Forensic Sci*. 1994; 39:123-128.

[28] Gunatilake, K., Goff, M. Detection of Organophosphate Poisoning In a Putrefying Body by Analyzing Arthropod Larvae. *J Forensic Sci*. 1989; 34:714-716.

[29] Greenberg, B., Kunich, J. C. *Entomology and the Law: Flies as Forensic Indicators*. Cambridge University Press, Cambridge. 1st ed. 2002; 1-306.

[30] Byrd, J. H., Lord, W. D., Wallace, J. R., Tomberlin, J. K. *Collection of entomological evidence during legal investigations*, pp. 127-176 In J. H. Byrd and J. L. Castner [eds], Forensic entomology: The utility of arthropods in legal investigations, 2nd edition. CRC Press, Florida, United States. 2010.

[31] Benecke, M. (2004) *Forensic Entomology: Arthropods and Corpses*. In: Tsokos M (ed.) Forensic Path Rev Vol II, Humana Press, Totowa (New Jersey, USA), pp. 207-240.

[32] Oliveira-Costa, J., de Mello-Patiu, C. A. Application of Forensic Entomology to estimate of the postmortem interval (PMI) in homicide investigations by the Rio de Janeiro Police Department in Brazil. *Aggrawal's Internet Journal of Forensic Medicine and Toxicology* 2004; 5(1):40-44.

[33] Goffa, M. L. *A Fly for the Prosecution (How Insect Evidence Helps Solve Crimes)*. Harvard University Press. 2000. Available at: https:// www.nytimes.com/books/first/g/gofffly.html (accessed on 18th May 2015).

[34] Joseph, I., Mathew, D. G., Sathyan, P., Vargheese, G. The use of insects in forensic investigations: An overview on the scope of forensic entomology. *J Forensic Dent Sci*. 2011:3(2):89-91.

[35] China Culture (2005). *The First Monographic Works on Forensic Medicine*: XiyuanJilu. Available at: http://www1.chinaculture.org/ created/2005-08/01/content_71484.htm.

[36] Catts, E. P., Goff, M. Forensic entomology in criminal investigations. *Annual Review of Entomology*, 1992; 37:253-272.

[37] McKnight B. E. (1981) *The washing away of wrongs: Forensic medicine in thirteenth-century China by Tz'u Sung*. Translated by McKnight, B. E. University of Michigan, Ann Arbor, p. 181.

[38] Anonymous. *On Maggots and Murders: Forensic Entomology*. Available at: http://www.nhm.ac.uk/resources-rx/files/22feat_maggots_ and_murders-7201.pdf (accessed on 26th August 2015).

[39] Mégnin, P. (1894). *La Faune des Cadavres*. Encyclopédie Scientifique des Aide-Memoire, p. 214, 28 figures, G. Masson, Gauthier-Villars et Fils, Paris.

[40] Haskell, N. H., Hall, R. D., Barnett, B., Muret, F. (1996). The use and value of entomological evidence during the murder investigation and subsequent pre-trial in Oklahoma. *20th Int. Cong. of Entomology*: 753.

[41] Lord, W. D., Burger, J. F. Collection and preservation of forensically important entomological materials. *J Forensic Sci*. 1983; 28:936-944.

[42] Catts, E. P., Haskell, N. H. *Entomology and Death: A procedural guide*. Joyce's Print Shop, South Carolina. 1st ed. 1990; 1-182.

[43] Haskell, N. H., Lord, W. D., Byrd, J. H. (2001) *Collection of entomological evidence during death investigations*. In: Byrd J. H., Castner J. L. (eds) Forensic entomology-the utility of arthropods in legal investigations. CRC Press, Boca Raton, FL, pp. 81-120.

[44] Henssge, C., Madea, B., Knight, B., Nokes, L., Krompecher, T. (1995). *The estimation of the Time since Death in the Early Postmortem Interval*. Arnold. p. 262.

[45] Kashyap, V. K., Pillai, V. V. Efficacy of entomological method in estimation of postmortem interval: a comparative analysis. *Forensic Science International*, 1989; 40:245-250.

[46] Nuorteva, P. *Sarcosaprophagous insects as forensic indicators*. In Forensic Medicine, a Study in Trauma and Environmental Hazards, Vol. II: Physical Trauma, Tedeschi C. G. W. B. Saunders Co., Philadelphia, London, Toronto. 1997; 3: 1072-1095.

[47] Anderson, G. S. (2001). *Insect succession on carrion and its relationship to determining time since death*, pp. 143-175. In J. H. Byrd and J. L. Castner (eds.), Forensic entomology: the utility of arthropods in legal investigations. CRC, Boca Raton, FL.

[48] Payne, J. A. A summer carrion study of the baby pig *Sus scrofa* Linnaeus. *Ecology*, 1965; 46:592-602.

[49] Reed, H. B. A study of dog carcass communities in Tennessee, with special reference to the insects. *The American Midland Naturalist*, 1958; 59:213-245.

[50] ASISTM. Forensic entomology. *Use of insects to help solve crime*. Available at: http://www.clt.uwa.edu.au/__data/assets/pdf_file/0015/2301612/fse07_forensic_entomology.pdf (accessed on 26th August 2015).

[51] Anderson, G. S (2009). *Factors that influence insect succession on carrion*. In: Byrd J. H., Castner J. L. (eds.) Forensic entomology: The utility of arthropods in legal investigations. 2nd ed. Boca Raton, FL: CRC Press, pp. 201-250.

[52] Smith, K. G. V. (1986). *A manual of forensic entomology*. London, UK: The British Museum (Natural History) and Cornell University Press.

[53] Ashworth, J. R., Wall, R. Responses of the sheep blowflies Luciliasericata and Lxuprina to odour and the development of semiochemical baits. *Med Vet Entomol*. 1994; 8:303-309.

[54] LeBlanc, H. N., Logan, J. G. *Exploiting Insect Olfaction in Forensic Entomology*. In: Amendt J., Goff M. L., Campobasso C. P., Grassberger M., editors. Current Concepts in Forensic Entomology. Netherlands: Springer; 2010. pp. 205-21.

[55] Tullis, K., Goff, M. L. Arthropod succession in exposed carrion in a tropical rainforest on O'ahu Island, Hawai. *J. Med. Entomol*. 1987; 24: 332-9.

[56] Carloye, L., Bambara, S. (2006). *Crime Solving Insects*. Available at: http://ipm.ncsu.edu/4-H/CSIfinal.pdf (accessed on 25th August 2015).

[57] Aspoas, B. R. Afrotropical *Sarcophagidae* in carrion fly community. *Med Vet Entomol*. 1994; 8:292-294.

[58] Anderson, G. S., Van Laerhoven, S. L. Initial studies on insect succession on carrion in Southwestern British Columbia. *J Forensic Sci* 1996; 41:617-625.

[59] Chua, T. H., Chong, Y. V. (2012). *Role of Polymerase Chain Reaction in Forensic Entomology, Polymerase Chain Reaction*, Dr Patricia Hernandez-Rodriguez (Ed.), ISBN: 978-953-51-0612-8.

[60] Anderson, G. S. *Practical Exercise in Forensic Entomology*, Gazette, 1996; 58(9):3-6.

[61] Amendt, J., Krettek, R., Zehner, R. Forensic entomology. *Naturwissenschaften*. 2004; 91:51-65.

[62] Lord, W. D. (1990) *Case histories of use of insects in investigations*. In Entomology and Death, A procedural guide. E. P. Catts and N. H. Haskell, Eds. Joyce's Print Shop, South Carolina. 1st ed. pp. 9-37.

[63] Lord, W. D., Rodriquez, W. C. *Forensic Entomology: The Use of Insects in the Investigation of Homicide and Untimely Death*. Prosecutor, 1989; 22(3):41-48.

[64] Schoenly, K., Reid, W. Dynamics of heterotrophic succession in carrion arthropod assemblages: discrete series or a continuum of change? *Oecologia* (Berlin) 1987; 73:192-202.

[65] Davies, L. Species composition and larval habitats of blowfly (*Calliphoridae*) populations in upland areas in England and Wales. *Med Vet Entomol*. 1990; 4:61-8.

[66] Schoenly, K., Goff, M. L., Wells, J. D., Lord, W. D. Quantifying statistical uncertainty in succession-based entomological estimates of the postmortem interval in death scene investigations: a simulation study. *Am. Entomol*. 1996; 42:106-112.

[67] Nuorteva, P., Isokoski, M., Laiho, K. Studies on the possibilities of using blowflies (Dipt.) as medicolegal indicators in Finland. I. Report of our indoor cases from the city of Helsinki. *Ann. Entomol. Fenn*. 1967; 33:217-225.

[68] Erzinclioglu, Y. U. The application of entomology to forensic medicine. *Med. Sci. Law* 1983; 23:57-63.

[69] Greenberg, B. (1973). *Flies and disease*, vol. II. Biology and disease transmission. Princeton Univ. Press, Princeton, New Jersey. p. 447.

[70] Goff, M. L., Odum, C. B. Forensic entomology in the Hawaiian Islands: three case studies. *Am. J. Forensic Med. Pathol* B 1987; 45-50.
[71] Catts, E. P. Problems in Estimating the Postmortem Interval in Death Investigations. *J. Agric. Entomol*. 1992; 9:4:245-255.

In: Law Enforcement and Crime
Editor: Emanuel T. Rhodes
ISBN: 978-1-63484-127-6


*Chapter 3*

# Child Fatality: The Utility of a Public Health Approach to Prevention Efforts

***Rohit Shenoi[1], MD, Samantha Mathew[2] and Angelo P. Giardino[1,3,*], MD, PhD***
[1]Texas Children's Hospital, Houston, Texas, US
[2]University of Houston, Houston, Texas, US
[3]Baylor College of Medicine, Houston, Texas, US

## Abstract

A child fatality is the death of a child caused by an injury resulting from abuse or neglect or where abuse or neglect was a contributing factor. It is estimated that there were 1,520 childhood deaths from abuse and neglect in the USA in 2013. Most victims are infants and the perpetrators are usually parents acting singly or together. A public health approach is likely to address the problem and involves four fundamental activities: (1) the surveillance of the injury; (2) identification of its risk factors and protective factors; (3) evaluation of interventions that reduce the injury burden and (4) dissemination and widespread adoption of best practices that are effective in decreasing the burden of injury. Child fatalities are an important but under-recognized problem related to under-reporting, lack of consistent standards for child autopsies, varying roles

* Corresponding Author: apgiardi@texaschildrenshospital.org.

and inadequate coordination of Child Protective Service agencies and investigating agencies and a lack of training of medical examiners in child abuse and neglect. Prevention of child fatalities requires a multidisciplinary, comprehensive approach that looks at data, takes action and promotes policy changes at the federal, state and local levels with the active engagement of families and their communities.

## INTRODUCTION

Homicide is defined as a death resulting from the use of physical force or power, threatened or actual, against another person, group, or community when a preponderance of evidence indicates that the use of force was intentional. It excludes vehicular homicide without intent to injure, unintentional firearm deaths, combat deaths or acts of war, and deaths of unborn fetuses. Homicide is the fourth leading cause of death for persons aged 1–14 years. It is highest in infants aged <1 year (8.2 deaths per 100,000 population) and lowest among children aged 5–14 years (CDC, 2009). In the United States, children under age two account for 48% of all homicides involving children 0 to 14 years of age (WISQARS, 2015). In this chapter, we will discuss the epidemiology of child homicides, disparities and policy implications and describe current interventions that have been successful in reducing the burden of inflicted child deaths. Homicides in youth, which have a different set of epidemiological factors and preventive strategies, is beyond the scope of this chapter and will not be discussed. We propose that a public health approach based on analysis of available empiric data coupled with targeted efforts at both the family and community levels holds the most promise towards reducing and ultimately eliminating child maltreatment related child homicides. The classic public health approach involves four steps:

1) the surveillance of the injury;
2) identification of its risk factors and protective factors;
3) evaluation of interventions that reduce the injury burden, and,
4) dissemination and widespread adoption of best practices that are effective in decreasing the burden of injury.

**Table 1a. Child Fatality Rates per 100,000 Children, 2009-2013**

| Year | Reporting States | Child Population of Reporting States | | National Fatality Rate per 100,000 Children | Child Population of all 52 States | National Estimate of Child Fatalities |
|---|---|---|---|---|---|---|
| 2009 | 51 | 73,234,095 | | 2.30 | 75,512,062 | 1,740 |
| 2010 | 52 | 75,016,501 | | 2.08 | 75,016,501 | 1,560 |
| 2011 | 51 | 73,364,309 | | 2.11 | 74,771,549 | 1,580 |
| 2012 | 50 | 72,885,656 | | 2.19 | 74,549,919 | 1,630 |
| 2013 | 50 | 72,744,718 | | 2.04 | 74,399,940 | 1,520 |

*Data are from the Child File and Agency File or the SDC. National fatality rates per 100,000 children were calculated by dividing the number of child fatalities by the population of reporting states and multiplying by 100,000.*

*If fewer than 52 states reported data, the national estimate of child fatalities was calculated by multiplying the national fatality rate by the child population of all 52 states and dividing by 100,000. The estimate was rounded to the nearest 10. If 52 states reported data, the national estimate of child fatalities was calculated by taking the number of reported child fatalities and rounding to the nearest 10. Because of the rounding rule, the national estimate could have fewer fatalities than the actual reported number of fatalities.*

U.S. Department of Health and Human Services, Administration for Children and Families, Administration on Children, Youth and Families, Children's Bureau (2015). *Child Maltreatment 2013*. Available from http://www.acf.hhs.gov/programs/cb/ research-data-technology/statistics-research/child-maltreatment.

# Table 1b. Child Fatalities, 2013

## By Sex

| Sex | Child Population | Child Fatalities Number | Child Fatalities Percent | Child Fatalities Rate per 100,000 Children |
|---|---|---|---|---|
| Boys | 29,972,380 | 706 | 58.0 | 2.36 |
| Girls | 28,670,323 | 507 | 41.7 | 1.77 |
| Unknown | | 4 | 0.3 | |
| **National** | **58,642,703** | **1,217** | **100.0** | |

*Based on data from 42 states. Rates are calculated by dividing the number of male child fatalities and female child fatalities by the child population for each sex and multiplying by 100,000. There are no population data for unknown sex and therefore, no rates.*

## By Race and Ethnicity

| Race | Child Population | Child Fatalities Number | Child Fatalities Percent | Child Fatalities Rate per 100,000 Children |
|---|---|---|---|---|
| SINGLE RACE | | | | |
| African-American | 8,301,186 | 375 | 33.0 | 4.52 |
| American Indian or Alaska Native | 491,084 | 14 | 1.2 | 2.85 |
| Asian | 2,004,063 | 13 | 1.1 | 0.65 |
| Hispanic | 11,483,277 | 165 | 14.5 | 1.44 |
| Pacific Islander | 85,808 | 4 | 0.4 | 4.66 |
| Unknown | | 61 | 5.4 | |
| White | 29,242,735 | 446 | 39.3 | 1.53 |
| MULTIPLE RACE | | | | |
| Two or More Races | 2,013,260 | 58 | 5.1 | 2.88 |
| **National** | **53,621,413** | **1,136** | **100.0** | |

*Based on data from 42 states. The category multiple race is defined as any combination of two or more race categories. Counts associated with specific racial groups (e.g., White) are exclusive and do not include Hispanic.*

*States with more than 45 percent of race or ethnicity as unknown or missing were excluded from this analysis. Rates were calculated by dividing the number of fatalities for each race or ethnicity by the child population for each race or ethnicity and multiplying by 100,000. This analysis includes only those states that reported both race and ethnicity.*

**By Sex**

| Sex | Child Population | Child Fatalities | | |
|---|---|---|---|---|
| | | Number | Percent | Rate per 100,000 Children |
| Boys | 29,972,380 | 706 | 58.0 | 2.36 |
| Girls | 28,670,323 | 507 | 41.7 | 1.77 |
| Unknown | | 4 | 0.3 | |
| **National** | **58,642,703** | **1,217** | **100.0** | |

*Based on data from 42 states. Rates are calculated by dividing the number of male child fatalities and female child fatalities by the child population for each sex and multiplying by 100,000. There are no population data for unknown sex and therefore, no rates.*

**By Race and Ethnicity**

| Race | Child Population | Child Fatalities | | |
|---|---|---|---|---|
| | | Number | Percent | Rate per 100,000 Children |
| **SINGLE RACE** | | | | |
| African-American | 8,301,186 | 375 | 33.0 | 4.52 |
| American Indian or Alaska Native | 491,084 | 14 | 1.2 | 2.85 |
| Asian | 2,004,063 | 13 | 1.1 | 0.65 |
| Hispanic | 11,483,277 | 165 | 14.5 | 1.44 |
| Pacific Islander | 85,808 | 4 | 0.4 | 4.66 |
| Unknown | | 61 | 5.4 | |
| White | 29,242,735 | 446 | 39.3 | 1.53 |
| **MULTIPLE RACE** | | | | |
| Two or More Races | 2,013,260 | 58 | 5.1 | 2.88 |
| **National** | **53,621,413** | **1,136** | **100.0** | |

*Based on data from 42 states. The category multiple race is defined as any combination of two or more race categories. Counts associated with specific racial groups (e.g., White) are exclusive and do not include Hispanic.*

*States with more than 45 percent of race or ethnicity as unknown or missing were excluded from this analysis. Rates were calculated by dividing the number of fatalities for each race or ethnicity by the child population for each race or ethnicity and multiplying by 100,000. This analysis includes only those states that reported both race and ethnicity.*

**Table 1b. (Continued)**

**By Maltreatment Types**

| Maltreatment Type | Child Fatalities | Maltreatment Types | |
|---|---|---|---|
| | | Number | Percent |
| Medical Neglect | | 105 | 8.6 |
| Neglect | | 869 | 71.4 |
| Other | | 282 | 23.2 |
| Physical Abuse | | 569 | 46.8 |
| Psychological Abuse | | 22 | 1.8 |
| Sexual Abuse | | 12 | 1.0 |
| Unknown | | 1 | 0.1 |
| **National** | **1,217** | **1,860** | **152.8** |

*Based on data from 45 states. A child may have suffered from more than one type of maltreatment and therefore, the total number of reported maltreatments exceeds the number of fatalities and the total percentage of reported maltreatments exceeds 100.0 percent. The percentages are calculated against the number of child fatalities in the reporting states.*

**With Selected Caregiver Risk Factors**

| Caregiver Risk Factor | Reporting States | Child Fatalities from Reporting States | Child Fatalities With a Caregiver Risk Factor | |
|---|---|---|---|---|
| | | | Number | Percent |
| Financial Problem | 26 | 700 | 63 | 9.0 |
| Domestic Violence | 32 | 949 | 146 | 15.4 |
| Public Assistance | 23 | 563 | 145 | 25.8 |

*For each caregiver risk factor, the analysis includes only those states that reported at least 1 percent of child victims' caregiver with the risk factor.*

*This table was changed for the Child Maltreatment 2013 report. This is the first time the poverty-related caregiver risk factor data have been presented in the Child Maltreatment report series.*

U.S. Department of Health and Human Services, Administration for Children and Families, Administration on Children, Youth and Families, Children's Bureau (2015). *Child Maltreatment 2013*. Available from http://www.acf.hhs.gov/programs/cb/research-data-technology/statistics-research/child-maltreatment.

More than 80 percent of child homicides are considered to be fatal child abuse (Overpeck, 1998; Herman-Giddens, 1999). Child abuse homicides are those where an act or a failure to act on the part of a guardian results in a child's death. According to the National Child Abuse and Neglect Data System

(NCANDS), in 2013, there were an estimated 1,520 childhood deaths due to abuse or neglect (Child Welfare Information Gateway, 2015). See Table 1a and 1b. Unfortunately the burden of child abuse deaths is higher since these deaths are under-reported (Herman-Giddens, 1999). It is more difficult to establish whether a fatality is due to neglect than if it is due to physical abuse. There are several reasons for the under-reporting (Table 2). One of the challenges in determining maltreatment as a cause for homicide is that this information is not readily identified through population-based epidemiological studies or service-based case recording systems. These deaths can be determined through mortality surveillance systems such as the medico-legal investigations of all known and suspected deaths from external causes and all unexpected deaths in young children.

**Table 2. Barriers affecting the accuracy and consistency of child fatality data (Child Welfare Information Gateway, 2015)**

| |
|---|
| Variation among reporting requirements and definitions of child abuse and neglect and other terms |
| Variation in death investigation systems and training |
| Variation in State child fatality review and reporting processes |
| The length of time (up to a year in some cases) it may take to establish abuse or neglect as the cause of death |
| Inaccurate determination of the manner and cause of death, resulting in the miscoding of death certificates; this includes deaths labeled as accidents, sudden infant death syndrome (SIDS), or "manner undetermined" that would have been attributed to abuse or neglect if more comprehensive investigations had been conducted |
| Limited coding options for child deaths, especially those due to neglect or negligence, when using the International Classification of Diseases to code death certificates |
| The ease with which the circumstances surrounding many child maltreatment deaths can be concealed or rendered unclear |
| Lack of coordination or cooperation among different agencies and jurisdictions |

Child Welfare Information Gateway (2015). *Child abuse and neglect fatalities 2013: Statistics and interventions.* Washington, DC: U.S. Department of Health and Human Services, Children's Bureau.

# EPIDEMIOLOGY

## Types of Homicide and Mechanisms of Death

In order to understand the epidemiology of child homicide, it is helpful to utilize a conceptual framework that addresses the causes of child mortality and explains the factors underpinning child abuse. The causes of child abuse are complex with many interconnecting influences. The human ecological model for human development described by Bronfenbrenner (1979) posits a dynamic adaptation of the developing human being to the changing properties of the immediate settings in which the person lives, with interacting factors existing at the 1) individual, 2) family, 3) neighborhood and 4) societal levels. The extent to which an individual is connected to his/her community is called social capital. It refers to the community resources available to the individual and that person's ability to utilize them. The greater an individual is engaged with his/her community, the greater the available system supports and the less likelihood of adverse childhood experiences. Prevention efforts, using this conceptual framework would then be oriented towards increasing an individual's and a family's social capital.

Sidebotham (2014) suggested four broad domains that impact child mortality. These include 1) biological and psychological factors intrinsic to the child, 2) factors in the physical environment, 3) factors in the social environment, and 4) factors that relate to service delivery. Socio-economic status is a very important factor that plays a role in all domains. While some factors are relatively fixed, such as gender, age, ethnicity, genetics and some parental characteristics, interventions that impact the physical and social environments and health service delivery could potentially decrease the burden of child maltreatment and have a positive impact on child fatality.

Moving on to the exploration of child death, five types of child fatalities emerge (Sidebotham, 2011). They include:

(1) severe physical assault,
(2) infanticide and covert homicide,
(3) extreme neglect or deprivation,
(4) deliberate or overt homicide, and
(5) death indirectly caused by maltreatment.

Severe physical assaults can include or exclude neglect, but typically consist of head injuries from shaking or other causes, abdominal injuries, and multiple types of injuries. This corresponds to Type 1 homicides described by Fujiwara, 2009. These usually occur through impulsive attacks and death may not be intended. Emergency care is often sought for the victims and victims are taken to the hospital. The explanations offered are inconsistent with the manner of death. The perpetrators are likely to use their hands rather than weapons. The second type of homicides (Type 2 per Fujiwara, 2009) includes assaults that result from firearms, beatings, stabbings, and strangulation. Infanticide and covert homicide involve less violent or less apparent methods, often perpetrated by the mother. This class of fatal maltreatment can include exposure, asphyxiation, drowning, strangulation, or poisoning with some degree of homicidal intent. Deaths can also involve circumstances in which the mother concealed the pregnancy and is the suspected perpetrator. The third type is extreme neglect that can occur through starvation, exposure, or a deliberate failure to respond to the child's medical needs. Deliberate homicides constitute the fourth type. These involve stabbings, firearms, and severe beatings with intent to kill, but the homicidal nature is more apparent. Cases can also involve sexual assaults, killings of multiple family members or of other individuals, murder-suicides, and arson. Finally, deaths indirectly caused by maltreatment often result from lack of adequate parental care and supervision and not from extreme or prolonged neglect. Sudden death in infancy or fatal accidents from drug ingestion, drownings, falls, electrocution, gunshot wounds, and fires are examples. Furthermore, deaths from natural causes in which parents did not seek medical attention and deaths from risk-taking activities (including substance abuse) in youths with a history of abuse can be classified as those indirectly caused by parental maltreatment. Suicides can also fit into this category (Sidebotham, 2011).

As described above, there are many mechanisms of death in child homicide. Homicides may occur due to abuse over a period of time or as a single impulsive incident. Deaths due to neglect occur due to omission of care and nurturing. The latter can be chronic such as chronic malnutrition or acute, such as that death due to leaving a child unsupervised in a dangerous environment, e.g., bath tub or hot car. Seventy two percent are due to neglect alone or in combination with another type of maltreatment; 47% due to physical abuse alone in combination with another maltreatment type and medical neglect alone or in combination is responsible for 9% of fatalities (Child Welfare Information Gateway, 2015). Typical locations for intentional injuries include the intracranial area, abdomen, and thorax. In addition, victims of maltreatment are younger and have a medical history prior to the injury (Discala, 2000). The most common cause of death is head trauma, followed by blunt force trauma to the body. Most injuries come from hands or feet, with no other weapon used. Most occur at home. Drowning and asphyxia are the other most important causes of death (de Silva, 1993, Shenoi, 2013).

Birken (2009) studied the influence of neighborhood income on child homicides among Canadian children living in urban areas. The age-adjusted relative risks for the lowest versus highest neighborhood income quintiles were 2.95 for all children < 15 years of age and 3.39 for children <5 years of age. The authors suggested that that effective child homicide-prevention strategies should be focused on children <5 years of age living in low-income areas.

Some researchers have studied the health utilization characteristics of abused children prior to abuse with the hope of identifying certain distinct characteristics. Higher emergency department (ED) use was observed in abused Utah children prior to their abuse diagnosis. Guenther (2009) and Friedlander (2005) observed that victims of serious and substantiated physical abuse and neglect change ambulatory care providers with greater frequency than non-abused children but there was no difference in frequency of ED visits prior to the abuse diagnosis. Both studies were unable to describe specific pattern of diagnoses or rates of diagnoses of injury or nonspecific somatic complaints. Shenoi (personal communication, 2015) observed that victims of child homicide have a higher number of EMS calls prior to their death than children who die from natural causes.

Racial differences in socioeconomic position (SEP) and maternal risk behaviors are believed to play a role in infant mortality. El-Sayed (2015) who studied a little over 2 million mother–child dyads in Michigan observed that SEP and maternal risk behaviors explained nearly a third of the disparity in infant mortality overall, and over 25% of disparities in several specific causes including homicide, accident, sudden infant death syndrome, and respiratory distress syndrome and disorders relating to short gestation and low birth weight. However, SEP and maternal risk behaviors had little influence on disparities in other specific causes, such as congenital anomalies. African American infants in the U.S. are almost three times more likely to die before reaching age one than are their non-Hispanic White counterparts. Socioeconomic status and maternal demographics such as birth out of wedlock, teen motherhood, use of alcohol during pregnancy, and access to prenatal care are significant predictors of infant mortality. Some of these risk factors, including lower access to prenatal care, lower socioeconomic status, and out-of-wedlock pregnancies, are more prevalent among African American mothers. They concluded that policies should focus towards addressing these disparities.

What does the foregoing suggest? There appears to be interconnectedness between crime and health disparity and poor social capital. In Chicago, more than 75% of census tracts with high homicide rates contain a high level of clustering for infant mortality and low birth weight (Sampson, 2003). These same neighborhoods also exhibit poverty, increased high school drop-out rates, and joblessness. What is concerning is that pediatric illnesses such as obesity, asthma, and unintentional injuries, are also increased in these areas (McClaine, 2011). There is a clear nexus between poverty, crime and ill health at the street level. Tackling this urban poverty and ill health requires interventions that dissect the factors that are responsible and offers solutions which address the problem in its entirety rather than the individual components. Pulling all this together and examining the data at hand, we can see potential targeted actions possible interventions and specific areas for attention, namely the:

***Victims:*** Young children, because of their dependency, small size, and inability to defend themselves constitute the most vulnerable group. Children under age three accounted for 74% of deaths (Child Welfare Information Gateway, 2015). Victims are most often male.

***Perpetrators:*** Individuals responsible for the care of children such as parents, acting alone or with another parent, account for 79% of fatalities. The mother acting alone (28%), father acting alone (12%), both parents (25%) and non-parents including day-care providers (17%) are the main perpetrators. The most typical perpetrator is a young adult in his or her mid-20s, without a high school diploma, living at or below the poverty level, depressed, and who may have difficulty coping with stressful situations. Fathers and mothers' boyfriends are most often the perpetrators in abuse deaths; mothers are more often at fault in neglect fatalities. Cavanaugh (2007) observed that fathers who murdered their children were undereducated, underemployed men with significant criminal history who perpetrated violence against their intimate partners.

***Parental Risk Factors:*** Risk factors associated with infant homicide include childbearing at an early age (age 19 years or younger) particularly if the mother has given birth previously (Overpeck, 1998). Parents of the victim are usually young, and/or unmarried mothers with low educational attainment. Other risk factors include previous abuse in the parent, unemployment parental stress, substance abuse and mental ill health and depression, family financial problems, and residing in households with unrelated male adults (Fujiwara 2009).

***Disparities:*** There are important disparities in child homicide worth noting. Child homicide is concentrated in population areas where there is a preponderance of minorities. African-Americans are highly represented. However, the role of race may not be as important as is socio-economic status. Shenoi (2013) evaluated the relationship between neighborhood sociodemographic factors, community resources, and homicides involving young children using spatial analysis of children under age five murdered in metropolitan Houston. Data on county population, household, socioeconomic, and residential mobility characteristics were allocated to census block groups. Age-adjusted spatial clusters of the homicides were identified. Child maltreatment accounted almost for all homicides (94%). In all, 64% of the homicides were concentrated in 12 age-adjusted spatial clusters involving 3% of county area. Predictors for number of homicides were a larger number of single-parent households (male and female) and lower median household income. Distance to nearest community resources was not significant. Spatial clusters of child homicides were associated with low-income neighborhoods and single-parent (male and female) households. No association between the spatial clusters of child homicides and their proximity to community resources was observed. A high percentage of child homicides were concentrated in a small area of the county, which offers the potential for targeted, cost-effective interventions.

## Community Response to Child Fatalities

In order to mount an appropriate response to combat child homicides, one must develop more accurate ways to classify and count maltreatment-related fatalities as a means of informing policy and practice as well as developing better child safety performance measures. As described earlier (Table 1), barriers in gaining an accurate assessment of child homicides include under-reporting, lack of consistent standards for child autopsies, varying roles of child protection agencies in investigating maltreatment fatalities, poor coordination between investigating agencies and lack of training of medical examiners or elected coroners in child maltreatment. To address these issues, multidisciplinary and multiagency child fatality review teams have emerged to provide a coordinated approach to understanding child deaths also supported by the 1992 reauthorization of the Child Abuse Prevention and Treatment Act

(CAPTA), which required States to include information on child death review (CDR) in their program plans. Child fatality review teams form an important entity that investigates these deaths (Giardino & Reece, 2005). Their members who all have an interest in the prevention of child homicides include coroners, police officers, social and legal workers, health care and public health officials, representatives from schools, and occasionally community members. Through systematic review of child deaths, using a formal multidisciplinary process, communities and their representative agencies are well positioned to collaborate on understanding the causes of death and then to take action in order to address that cause and prevent future child fatalities (Giardino & Reece, 2005).

## Prevention of Child Maltreatment Related Fatalities: A Public Health Approach

Since most child homicides are due to maltreatment, a reduction in child abuse will reduce the number of child homicides. Also, since there are different types of child abuse, the interventions to reduce child maltreatment homicide may differ from one another. Certain key observations are worth noting. First, as Cavanaugh (2007) observed, while child protection professionals work hard to provide services to children and families, fathers as the perpetrators of such assaults do not receive much attention in policy and practice. Most interventions target mothers (who are involved in only 11% of homicides) rather than the vast majority of perpetrators who are male. Second, the prevention of child maltreatment has traditionally focused on the involvement of social services for the treatment and rehabilitation of victims and their families and the criminal justice system for punishing perpetrators. While this is crucial, these methods have been insufficient in eradicating the problem.

A public health approach that is grounded in population health principles has been suggested to reduce the burden of child abuse and neglect. This approach involves four steps: (1) the surveillance of the injury; (2) identification of its risk factors and protective factors; (3) evaluation of interventions that reduce the injury burden and (4) dissemination and widespread adoption of best practices that are effective in decreasing the burden of injury. This model has been particularly successful in unintentional childhood injury prevention such as bicycle helmet use to prevent brain injury and measures to promote supine sleeping to prevent sudden infant death. The public health model will require a comprehensive approach that targets local communities and ensures their active participation with support from the greater community, local and state governing bodies. In addition, a multilayered level of prevention with cross-sector involvement is essential in addressing this problem. The components should involve the individual, the family, the community, service systems, and public policy, as well as addressing broader public attitudes and beliefs (Richmond-Crum, 2013). A broad community response could involve health, law enforcement, and education, as well as child welfare systems and service providers with the support of the media, elected officials, the broader public, and anti-poverty and affordable housing experts and activists. A public health perspective is more cost-effective and wide-reaching in scope compared to individualized interventions. Social services cannot be offered to every family. Furthermore, the average cost of maltreatment for medical and non-medical expenses is $100,000 per child. Training practitioners, on the other hand, could cost as little as $11.74 per child.

A suggested framework as enunciated by Haddon (1970) offers four levels of prevention: a) Primary prevention which targets the unaffected or pre-affected population and where all persons are included regardless of their decision to participate; b) Secondary prevention that is directed towards the at-risk population; c) Tertiary prevention that is directed to those who are already affected or injured with an additional category d) Quaternary prevention that attempts to reduce the disease and the risk factors of the disease by changing public policy.

- Primary Prevention: Primary intervention involves methods and policies to protect children from abuse. It incorporates public health initiatives such as parenting classes, child safety education, parent-child therapy, and home visitations. Furthermore, attention to socioeconomic issues is very important in addressing the circumstance surrounding child abuse. Access to education and economic opportunity for marginalized, low-income communities empowers adults and provides a healthier social structure for children. Removing environmental risks in the neighborhood can improve a child's physical health and quality of life. Finally, changing cultural attitudes particularly with regards to women and children can reduce domestic abuse occurrences. Laws are needed to enforce protections for women, children, minorities, and low-income adults. Vigilance from the medical community is also required for screenings for parental mental illness or substance abuse, detection of abusive head trauma, and primary care guidance for new parents. Background screenings are essential to protect children from those with a history of violence or abuse.

- Secondary Prevention: This strategy alerts officials to the crime and rescues the child from the situation. Strong organization between hotlines, emergency response teams, law enforcement officers, welfare workers, and crisis centers is necessary to ensure that the victim's needs are met at every step of the intervention. An integrated system is needed for appropriate referrals and follow-ups. Also, accurate reporting of information can help with the prosecution process.
- Tertiary Prevention: These measures provide therapy for victims (which may also include the mother and other family members) and prosecution for perpetrators. Tertiary prevention may also aim to prevent future abuse incidents by registering the offender and removing the person from employment, especially in child care capacities. Infrastructure development of EMS, emergency departments, rehabilitation facilities, and counseling services is optimal to provide holistic service to families affected by domestic abuse. The legal system should identify and appropriately punish perpetrators of abuse in order to protect victims in a timely manner.
- Quaternary Prevention: This level of prevention provides attempts to reduce the disease and the risk factors of the disease by changing public policy.

Since resources, both human and financial are precious and frequently limited or constrained by budgetary pressures, using the best evidence available to select the initiatives or programs with the highest likelihood of successfully reducing the risk for child maltreatment is essential to responsible practice. Table 3 summarizes the different interventions that have been found to be helpful in reducing the morbidity and mortality resulting from child maltreatment.

The Table uses an evidence-based approach to classifying the various programs and initiatives grouping them in the following categories: 1) strong evidence, 2) promising evidence, 3) need additional evaluation and 4) insufficient evidence as yet to demonstrate success.

**Table 3. Different Interventions found to be helpful in reducing morbidity and mortality resulting from child maltreatment***

| **Strong Evidence of Effectiveness; Highly Recommended; Best Practice** | |
|---|---|
| Intervention | More Information |
| Early Childhood Home Visiting Programs - Nurse-Family Partnership (Nurse Family Partnership, 2015; Olds, Henderson, Cole, et al., 1997; Olds, Henderson, Cole, et al., 1998; Kitzman, Olds, Henderson, et al., 1997; Olds, Kitzman, Hanks, et al., 2007; Olds, Robinson, O'Brien, et al., 2002; Olds, Robinson, Pettitt, et al., 2004.) | Trained personnel who visit high risk parents and children at home during the child's first two years of life and provide some combination of information, support, or training about child health, development, and care. Home visitation programs decrease the likelihood of child maltreatment by:<br>• Providing parents with guidance for caring and constructive interaction with their young children<br>• Facilitating the development of parental life skills<br>• Strengthening social support<br>• Linking families with social services<br>The demonstrated level of effectiveness of NFP is unsurpassed in evidence-based home visitation programs for the prevention of child maltreatment. Rigorous evaluation in randomized controlled trials (RCT) have shown consistent effects in reducing reports of maltreatment and associated outcomes. |
| Parent Skills Training – Triple P (Positive Parenting Program) (Triple P, 2015; Prinz, 2009; Prinz, Sanders, Shapiro, et al., 2009.) | Designed as a population based health approach to parenting using a multilevel system of parenting interventions based on need. The program is designed to prevent, as well as treat, behavioral and emotional problems in children and teenagers. Parenting programs are focused, short-term interventions aimed at improving parenting practices and may therefore be useful in the treatment of physically abusive or neglectful parenting. Triple P has shown positive effects on maltreatment and associated outcomes. |
| Enhanced Pediatric Clinic Care – Safe Environment for Every Kid (SEEK)(SEEK Project, 2015; Dubowitz, Feigelman, Lane, Kim, 2009; Dubowitz, Lane, Semiatin, Madger, 2012.) | The SEEK questionnaire screens parents of children ages 0–5 in pediatric primary care settings to identify exposure to intimate partner violence, mental illness, or substance abuse and provides appropriate referrals. Shows promise in both high and low risk populations. |
| School-based Early Childhood Intervention – Child-Parent Centers (Promising Practices Network, 2015; Reynolds, Temple, Ou, Robertson, et al., 2007.) | Comprehensive school-based education and family support to at-risk children and their parents. The program requires parental participation and emphasizes child-centered, individualized approaches to social and cognitive development. Evaluation results have shown reduction in child maltreatment among participants. |

| Promising Research Evidence | |
|---|---|
| Intervention | More Information |
| Early Childhood Home Visiting Programs – Early Start (Ferguson, Grant, Horwood, Ridder, 2005; Gonzalez, MacMillan, 2008.) | Nurses and social workers collaboratively work with at-risk families to generate solutions to family challenges, thereby fostering a partnership between the home visitor and client.<br>The goals of the program include: Improving child health and parenting skills; reducing maltreatment; supporting parental physical and mental health; promoting family economic well-being; and supporting stable, positive partner relationships. One RCT of the program has shown reduced rates of parental reports of severe abuse. |
| Early Childhood Home Visiting Programs – Parents as Teachers (Parents as Teachers, 2015; Avellar, Paulsell, Sama-Miller, Del Grosso, 2014.) | Parents as Teachers involves the training and certification of parent educators who work with families to strengthen protective factors and ensure that children are healthy, safe, and ready to learn. Study shows promising evidence that Parents as Teachers increases protective factors that can influence child maltreatment prevention. |
| Early Childhood Home Visiting Programs – SafeCare (National SafeCare Training and Research Center, 2015; Chaffin, Hecht, Bard, Silovsky, Beasely, 2012.) | Home parenting program that targets risk factors for child neglect and physical abuse in which parents are taught how to interact in a positive manner with their children and respond appropriately to challenging child behaviors, to recognize hazards in the home in order to improve the home environment, and to recognize and respond to symptoms of illness and injury. In a RCT of parents with a history of physically maltreating their child(ren), the intervention reduced the recidivism of future maltreatment. |
| Abusive Head Trauma Education Programs –<br>The Period of PURPLE Crying (Barr, 2015; Barr, Barr, Fujiwara, Conway, Catherine, Brant, 2009; Barr, Rivara, Barr, Cummings, Taylor et al., 2009.) | The program educates parents and caregivers on normal infant crying, the leading trigger for shaking an infant. The program is designed to be used primarily in universal, primary prevention settings, but is applicable to secondary prevention as well. The letters in PURPLE stand for the common properties of crying, including inconsolable crying, in infants. RCTs showed change in knowledge regarding newborn crying patterns, dangers of shaking an infant in response to crying, intent to walk away during inconsolable crying, and more likely to share information with caregivers. |

**Table 3. (Continued)**

| **Promising Research Evidence** | |
|---|---|
| Intervention | More Information |
| Kinship-care (Winokur, Holtan, Batchelder. 2014.) | Kinship care is a viable out-of-home placement option for children removed from the home for maltreatment. Current best evidence suggests that children in kinship foster care may do better than children in traditional foster care in terms of behavioral development, mental health functioning, and placement stability. However, this conclusion is tempered by the pronounced methodological and design weaknesses of the included studies. |
| Parent-Child Interaction Therapy (PCIT) (PCIT International, 2015; Terao, 1999; Chaffin, Silovsky, Funderburk, et al., 2004.) | Therapy with emphasis on improving parental skills to provide a nurturing and secure relationship and changing parent-child interaction patterns to increase their children's desirable behaviors, and decrease negative behaviors. PCIT has shown effective among families with history of physical abuse and neglect to reduce future maltreatment. |
| Cognitive Behavioral Therapy – Combined Parent-Child (Kilko, 1996.) | The program is grounded in cognitive behavioral theory. It is a short-term, strength-based therapy program for children ages 3-17 and their parents with goals to reduce children's PTSD symptoms, depression, other internalizing symptoms, and behavior problems, improve parental coping skills and parenting skills, increase parental empathy for children by enhancing insight into the impact their parenting behavior and interactions have on their children emotionally and behaviorally, increase positive parenting skills, enhance parent-child relationships, and reduce current and future use of corporal punishment by parents. |
| **Need Additional Evaluation** | |
| Abusive Head Trauma Education Programs - The Upstate New York Shaken Baby Syndrome Education Program (Dias, 2005.) | Parents of new infants receive written and video materials about Shaken Baby Syndrome (SBS) before leaving the hospital. Education about the normalcy of infant crying, the dangers of violent infant shaking, how to calm a crying infant and reduce caregiver frustration and anger, and how to wisely select other caregivers for the infant. Parents are asked to voluntarily sign a commitment statement affirming their receipt and understanding of the material. This program showed promising evidence in New York, however attempts to replicate in Pennsylvania with the same methods had null hypothesis results. |

| Need Additional Evaluation (continued) | |
|---|---|
| Intervention | More Information |
| Education of Clinicians to Recognize and Diagnose Abusive Injury (Carter, Bannon, Limbert, Docherty, Barlow, 2006; Louwers, Affourtit, Moll, de Koning, Korfage, 2010.) | Child protection training to influence professional knowledge, attitudes, and behavior in relation to child protection issues (unclear if training results in improved management of child abuse cases). Also training or procedural supports (checklists, flow diagrams) for clinicians designed to improve their recording, recognition, and appropriate response to cases of suspected child maltreatment – these are generally associated with improvements in the recording of child protection issues and raising awareness among health professionals — the impact of these changes on the actual recognition and diagnosis of child abuse is unknown. |
| Prevent exposure to intimate partner violence (IPV) (Nelson, Nygren, McInerney, Klein, 2004; Wathen, MacMillan, 2003.) | Screening women of childbearing age for Intimate Partner Violence. A direct means to prevent children's exposure to IPV is through prevention of violence itself. |
| Early Childhood Home Visiting Programs - Healthy Families America (Home Visiting for Prevention of Child Abuse and Neglect) (Olds, Kitzman, Hanks, et al., 2007; Fergusson, Grant, Horwood, Ridder, 2005; Duggan, Fuddy, Burrell, Higman, et al., 2004.) | Paraprofessional home visiting program model designed to work with overburdened families who are at risk for child abuse and neglect and other adverse childhood experiences. Build and sustain community partnerships to systematically engage overburdened families in home visiting services prenatally or at birth. Cultivate and strengthen nurturing parent-child relationships. Promote healthy childhood growth and development. Enhance family functioning by reducing risk and building protective factors (Lacking evidence for prevention of child abuse, however, well-supported by research evidence for promotion of child well-being). |
| **Insufficient Evidence** | |
| Primary care interventions to prevent child maltreatment (Moyer, 2013.) | The evidence on interventions in primary care to prevent child maltreatment among children without signs or symptoms of maltreatment is insufficient, and the balance of benefits and harms cannot be determined. |

* Table adapted from work by Cary Cain, RN, MPH, Marcellla Donaruma-Kwoh, MD, and Rohit Shenoi, MD.

Since a complete description of the different methods that have been used to combat child maltreatment and thereby reduce child homicides is very lengthy, the reader is requested to refer to the bibliography for more complete information.

## Conclusion

Child homicide involving young children is an important public health problem with child maltreatment being a principal cause. Most occur due to severe physical assault through impulsive actions on the part of the perpetrator. Child homicide is the fourth leading cause of death for persons aged 1–14 years, highest in infants aged <1 year (8.2 deaths per 100,000 population) and lowest among children aged 5–14 years (CDC, 2009). Children under age two account for 48% of all homicides involving children 0 to 14 years of age (WISQARS, 2015). More than 80 percent of child homicides are considered to be fatal child abuse (Overpeck, 1998; Herman-Giddens, 1999) and in 2013, an estimated 1,520 childhood deaths occurred due to abuse or neglect (Child Welfare Information Gateway, 2015). Child fatalities due to child maltreatment are more prevalent in areas of low family income and reduced social capital and complex familial, social and community issues are involved. The human ecological model for human development described by Bronfenbrenner (1979) that examines the changing properties of the immediate settings in which the person lives, is well suited as a conceptual framework from which to further understand the interacting factors that exist at the individual, family, neighborhood, and broader societal levels. This combined with a public health approach using the classic four steps of, 1) surveillance of the injury, identification of risk and protective factors, evaluation of interventions that reduce the injury burden, and, the dissemination of best practices has great potential to reduce and eventually eliminate child fatalities from child maltreatment. A multilayered level of prevention with cross-sector involvement is essential in addressing this problem (Richmond-Crum, 2013). What is needed is a “call to action” that generates a substantial response on the part of health, law enforcement, and education, as well as child welfare with the support of the media, elected officials, the general public, along with anti-poverty and affordable housing advocates. Pursuing evidence-based initiatives along with promising practices and a commitment to rigorous measurement and evaluation provides the path forward for effective action that is fiscally responsible but which allows us to pursue prevention to effectively tackle the need to address child homicide and fatalities due to child maltreatment.

# REFERENCES

Avellar S, Paulsell D, Sama-Miller E, Del Grosso P. Home visiting evidence of effectiveness review: Executive summary. Office of Planning, Research and Evaluation, Administration for Children and Families, U.S. Department of Health and Human Services. Washington, DC. 2014.

Barr M. Period of PURPLE Crying. Accessed online at http://purplecrying.info/what-is-the-period-of-purple-crying.php. Accessed on July 16, 2015.

Barr RG, Barr M, Fujiwara T, Conway J, Catherine N, Brant R. Do educational materials change knowledge and behavior about crying and shaken baby syndrome: a randomized controlled trial. *CMAJ.* 2009;180(7)727-733.

Barr RG, Rivara FP, Barr M, Cummings P, Taylor J, Lengua LJ, Meredith-Benitz E. Effectiveness of educational materials designed to change knowledge and behaviors regarding crying and shaken-baby syndrome in mothers of newborns: a randomized, controlled trial. *Pediatrics.* 2009;123:972-980.

Birken CS, Parkin PC, To, T, Wilins R, Macarthur C. *Neighborhood Socioeconomic Status and Homicides among Children in Urban Canada Pediatrics* 2009;123;e815-e819.

Bronfenbrenner, U. (1979). *The ecology of human development.* Cambridge, MA: Harvard University Press.

Carter YH, Bannon MJ, Limbert C, Docherty A, Barlow J. Improving child protection: a systematic review of training and procedural interventions. *Arch Dis Child.* 2006;91(9):740-743.

Cavanaugh K, Emerson Dobash R, Dobash RP. The murder of children by fathers in the context of child abuse *Child Abuse & Neglect* 31 (2007); 731–746.

Centers for Disease Control and Prevention (2009). *Surveillance for Violent Deaths —National Violent Death Reporting System,* 16 States, 2006 March 20, 2009. MMWR 2009; 58 (No. SS-1).

Chaffin M, Hecht D, Bard D, Silovsky, JF, Beasley WH. A statewide trial of the SafeCare home-based services model with parents in child protective services. *Pediatrics.* 2012;129(3):509-515.

Chaffin M, Silovsky JF, Funderburk B, et al. Parent-child interaction therapy with physically abusive parents: efficacy for reducing future reports. *J Consul Clin Psychol.* 2004;72:500-510.

Child Welfare Information Gateway (2015). *Child abuse and neglect fatalities 2013: Statistics and interventions.* Washington, DC: U.S. Department of Health and Human Services, Children's Bureau.

De Silva, S, & Oates, RK. (1993). Child homicide–the extreme of child abuse. *The Medical Journal of Australia*, 158(5), 300-301.

Dias, MS, Smith, K, deGuehery, K, Mazur, P, Li, V, & Shaffer, ML Preventing abusive head trauma among infants and young children: A hospital-based parent education program. *Pediatrics.* 2005;115:e470-477.

DiScala, C, Sege, R, Li, G, & Reece, RM Child abuse and unintentional injuries: a 10-year retrospective. *Arch Ped Adolesc Med.* 2000;154(1), 16-22.

Dubowitz H, Feigelman S, Lane W, Kim J, Pediatric primary care to help prevent child maltreatment: the Safe Environment for Every Kid (SEEK) Model. *Pediatrics.* 2009;123(3):858-864.

Dubowitz H, Lane WG, Semiatin JN, Magder LS. The SEEK model of pediatric primary care: can child maltreatment be prevented in a low-risk population? *Acad Pediatr.* 2012; Jul-Aug;12(4):259-68.

Duggan A, Fuddy L, Burrell L, Higman S, McFarlane E, Windham A, Sia C. Randomized trial of a statewide home visiting program: Impact in reducing parental risk factors. *Child Abuse & Neglect.* 2004;28:623-643.

El-Sayed, AM, Finkton, DW, Paczkowski, M, Keyes, KM, & Galea, S. Socioeconomic position, health behaviors, and racial disparities in cause-specific infant mortality in Michigan, USA. *Preventive medicine,* 2015;76, 8-13.

Fergusson DM, Grant H, Horwood LJ, Ridder EM. Randomized trial of the Early Start program of home visitation. *Pediatrics.* 2005;116:e803-809.

Friedlaender, EY, Rubin, DM, Alpern, ER, Mandell, DS, Christian, CW, & Alessandrini, EA. Patterns of health care use that may identify young children who are at risk for maltreatment. *Pediatrics,* 2005; 116(6), 1303-1308.

Fujiwara, T, Barber, C, Schaechter, J, & Hemenway, D. (2009). Characteristics of infant homicides: findings from a US multisite reporting system. *Pediatrics,* 124(2), e210-e217.

Giardino, AP, Reece, RM Child Fatality Review Team. *Child Maltreatment* (3rd Edition). G. W. Medical Publication: St. Louis, MO. 2005. pp. 805-852.

Gonzalez, A, MacMillan, HL. Preventing child maltreatment: an evidence-based update. *Symposium: Violence Against Children and Women.* 2008;54(4):280-286.

Guenther, E, Knight, S, Olson, LM, Dean, J.M, & Keenan, H.T(2009). Prediction of child abuse risk from emergency department use. *The Journal of pediatrics,* 154(2), 272-277.

Haddon W, Jr. On the escape of tigers: an ecologic note. *Am J Public Health.* 1970;60: 2229-2234.

Herman-Giddens ME, Brown G, Verbiest S et al. Underascertainment of Child Abuse Mortality in the United States. *JAMA.* 1999;282(5):463-467.

Kitzman H, Olds DL, Henderson CR Jr, et al. Effect of prenatal and infancy home visitation by nurses on pregnancy outcomes, childhood injuries, and repeated childbearing. A randomized controlled trial. *JAMA.* 1997;278:644-652.

Kolko D. Clinical monitoring of treatment course in child physical abuse: psychometric characteristics and treatment comparisons. *Child Abuse and Neglect.* 1996;20(1):23-43.

Louwers ECFM, Affourtit MJ, Moll HA, de Koning HJ, Korfage IJ. Screening for child abuse at emergency departments: a systematic review. *Arch Dis Child.* 2010;95:214-218.

McClaine, RJ, Garcia, V/F.(2011). Unnatural causes: Social determinants of child health and well-being. *Archives of Pediatrics & Adolescent Medicine,* 165, 476.

Moyer VA. Primary Care Interventions to Prevent Child Maltreatment: U.S. Preventive Services Task Force Recommendation Statement. *Ann Intern Med.* 2013;159:289-295.

National SafeCare Training and Research Center. Accessed online at http://safecare.publichealth.gsu.edu/. Accessed on July 16, 2015

Nelson HD, Nygren P, McInerney Y, Klein J. US Preventive Services Task Force. Screening women and elderly adults for family and intimate-partner violence: a review of the evidence for the US Preventive Services Task Force. *Ann Intern Med.* 2004;140:387-396.

Nurse-Family Partnership: Helping first-time parents succeed. Accessed online at http://www.nursefamilypartnership.org/. Accessed on July 16, 2015

Olds D, Henderson CR Jr, Cole R, et al. Long-term effects of home visitation on maternal life course and child abuse and neglect. Fifteen-year follow-up of a randomized trial. *JAMA.* 1997;278:637-643.

Olds D, Henderson CR Jr, Cole R, et al. Long-term effects of nurse home visitation on children's criminal and antisocial behavior: 15-year follow up of a randomized controlled trial. *JAMA.* 1998;280:1238-1244.

Olds DL, Kitzman H, Hanks C, et al. Effects of nurse home visiting on maternal and child functioning: age-9 follow-up of a randomized trial. *Pediatrics.* 2007;120:e832-845.

Olds DL, Robinson J, O'Brien R, Et al. Home visiting by paraprofessionals and by nurses: a randomized controlled trial. *Pediatrics.* 2002;110:486-496.

Olds DL, Robinson J, Pettitt L, et al. Effects of home visits by paraprofessionals and by nurses: age 4 follow-up results of a randomized trial. *Pediatrics.* 2004;114:1560-1568.

Overpeck MD, Brenner RA, Trumble AC, Trifiletti LB, Berendes HW. Risk factors for infant homicide in the United States. *N Engl J Med* 1998;339:1211-6.

Parents as Teachers. Accessed online at http://www.parentsasteachers.org/. Accessed on July 16, 2015

PCIT International. Accessed online at http://www.pcit.org/. Accessed on July 16, 2015.

Prinz R. dissemination of a multilevel evidence-based system of parenting interventions with broad application to child welfare populations. *Child Welfare.* 2009;88(1):127-132.

Prinz RJ, Sanders MR, Shapiro CJ, Whitaker DJ, Lutzker JR. Population-based prevention of child maltreatment: the U.S. Triple P system population trial. *Prev Sci.* 2009;115:e470-477.

Reynolds AJ, Temple JA, Ou SR, Robertson DL, et al. Effect of a school-based, early childhood intervention on adult health and well-being: a 19-year follow-up of low-income families. *Arch Pediatr Adolesc Med.* 2007;161(8):730-739.

Richmond-Crum M1, Joyner C, Fogerty S, Ellis ML, Saul J.Applying a public health approach: the role of state health departments in preventing maltreatment and fatalities of children. *Child Welfare.* 2013;92(2):99-117.

Sampson RJ. The neighborhood context of well-being. *Perspect Biol Med.* 2003; 46(3)(suppl):S53-S64.

SEEK Project. University of Maryland Medical Center. Accessed online at http://umm.edu/programs/childrens/services/child-protection/seek-project. Accessed on July 16, 2015.

Shenoi R. *Emergency medical service utilization by victims of child homicide.* Personal communication 2015.

Shenoi, R, Levine, N, Donaruma-Kwoh, MM, Lyn, MA, Hunter, JV, & Giardino, AP. (2013). The spatial relationship of child homicides to community resources in a large metropolitan area. *Sage open,* 3(2), 2158244013483132.

Sidebotham, P, Bailey, S, Belderson, P, & Brandon, M. (2011). Fatal child maltreatment in England, 2005–2009. *Child Abuse & Neglect,* 35(4), 299-306.

Sidebotham P, Fraser J, Covington T et al. Child death in high-income countries 3. Understanding why children die in high-income countries. *Lancet* 2014; 384: 915–27.

Terao SY. *Treatment effectiveness of parent-child interaction therapy with physically abusive parent-child dyads.* Stockton, California: University of the Pacific: 1999.

Triple P Implementation. Accessed online at http://www.triplep.net/. Accessed on July 16, 2015.

U.S. Department of Health and Human Services, Administration for Children and Families, Administration on Children, Youth and Families, Children's Bureau. (2015). *Child Maltreatment 2013.* Available from http://www.acf.hhs.gov/programs/cb/research-data-technology/statistics-research/child-maltreatment

Wathen CN, MacMillan HL. Interventions for violence against women: scientific review. *JAMA.* 2003;289:589-600.

Winokur M, Holtan A, Batchelder KE. Kinship care for the safety, permanency, and well-being of children removed from the home for maltreatment. Campbell Systematic Reviews. 2014;2.

WISQARS available at http://webappa.cdc.gov/sasweb/ncipc/mortrate10_us.html Accessed on August 16, 2015.

In: Law Enforcement and Crime
Editor: Emanuel T. Rhodes
ISBN: 978-1-63484-127-6


*Chapter 4*

# PRISON INFORMERS: THE PROSPECTS OF THE USE OF THEM IN POLAND

***Piotr Herbowski*** *

Assistant Professor, Department of Criminal Law, Faculty in Poznań, University of Social Sciences and Humanities, Poznań, Poland

## ABSTRACT

This chapter is devoted to cooperation between police forces and personal sources of information, recognized as one of the most important methods of operational work. The necessity of taking corrective actions in this area in Poland has been noticed for many years because, without efficiently functioning network of informants, it is difficult to imagine the effective implementation of operational actions for example those ones against organized crime groups. An important part in this system can be prison informants who collect information from detainees in detention centers or prisons. This category of sources has not been analyzed yet, and there is no doubt that penitentiary institutions can be a source of valuable knowledge about various crime groups. It may concern for instance illegal contacts between criminals, their attempts to affect the course of criminal processes or their managing criminal activities by inmates coming from organized crime groups. Prison informants, however, are perceived very negatively in Poland, which is certainly

* Corresponding author: Assistant Professor, Department of Criminal Law, Faculty in Poznań, University of Social Sciences and Humanities, Poznań, Poland, E-mail: piotr.herbowski@wp.pl.

influenced by past experience. Apart from this, there are a lot of difficulties connected with the cooperation with personal sources of information and the lack of appropriate regulations. Thus, nowadays, there are few perspectives of collecting valuable knowledge from prison informants in a large scale.

**Keywords:** personal sources of information, prison informants, police forces, organized crime

## Introduction

An issue which is rarely paid attention to, in the context of a discussion about operational and reconnaissance actions (Bulsiewicz 1997), is a cooperation with personal sources of information (Bulsiewicz 1992; Netczuk 2001; Netczuk 2006; Netczuk 2010). Confidentiality of its legal regulations, however, should not restrict analyses only to some aspects as it is one of the most important methods in operational work (Hanausek 2001; Kolejwa 1984). It is necessary to focus on what is deliberately hidden from the public, and what is wrongly assessed as leading to weakening the credibility of state services and, consequently, made confidential (Bulsiewicz 1997). One of such issues is an institution of prison informers. By presenting it, it is possible to create a wider picture of penitentiary reality (Cenckiewicz 2011) hiding behind the curtain of understatement. Making the subject of these deliberations the cooperation of the police with people who are not police officers – informers also defined as personal sources of information, resulted from the fact that information gained from them is highly valuable. Also, it often simplifies detection and evidentiary processes (Kolejwa 1984). During operational and reconnaissance actions carried out by the Polish police it can collect classified information, check, store and process it (Ustawa o Policji 1990). Article 22 of the Police Act seems a key one which states that the police when carrying out their duties can be assisted by persons who are not police officers. The assistance can be financially rewarded with the money from an operational fund of the police. The rules of creating and managing this fund are determined, in accordance with Article 22.3 of this Act, by the minister responsible for internal affairs.

## Operational and Reconnaissance Actions in Penitentiary Institutions

In Poland, the necessity of making the existing reconnaissance system more efficient has been pointed out for many years. First of all, it is needed to create an efficiently working system of informers in criminal circles (Hanausek 2001), especially in organized criminal groups. One of the important elements of this system could be obtaining information from inmates in penitentiaries. In literature, there are postulates of the re-use of prison informers. Giving up the above mentioned idea was caused by a collision with a correctional function of penitentiaries. It has been pointed out that the benefits resulted from introducing surveillance of inmates in countries of Western Europe (Young – sook Kim 1991; Mirfield 1997), justify considering the necessity of a participation of the Prison Service in the investigative work (Netczuk 2010). These postulates are not correct as they ignore the fact that prison informers have never completely stopped their work. The example known from the media concerns actions of an informer collaborating with the police and then with the Central Bureau of Anti-Corruption whilst investigating corruption amongst officers of the Prison Service. During the trial he testified against the former Chief of Regional Prison Service in Katowice colonel Włodzimierz W. – the highest rank official of this unit who, as a consequence, was arrested (Informacja, 2008).

In the current legal status the Prison Service has no authorization to carry out operational and reconnaissance actions and the right arguments against these actions were presented by Pomiankiewicz (2006) – the former Chief of The Central Board of Prison Service. He pointed out that the Prison Service is not prepared for this neither from an organizational nor staff point of view and its current power is sufficient enough to recognize moods and atmosphere among inmates and also to take right countermeasures. In turn, in acts entitling the relevant departments to such actions there is the lack of any restrictions connected with the place or area of their execution. This allows to apply for their legal admissibility in penitentiaries (Cempura 2011). This chapter, however, will focus exclusively on the prospects of the use of prison informers by the police. The problem of the admissibility of operational and reconnaissance actions in detention centers and prisons and the necessary cooperation of the Prison Service with institutions executing them, requires a separate study because a confidential letter written by the Chief of Central

Board of Prison Service in 2006 should be considered in this respect as insufficient (Pismo, 2006).

## Are Prison Informers Needed?

For many years penitentiary institutions have been rightly considered as a source of valuable knowledge about criminals and their interactions with the prison environment and the one outside this institution (Young – sook Kim 1991), especially about:

- illegal contacts,
- attempts to influence the course of criminal proceedings,
- targeting criminal activity by inmates,
- planning new offences,
- the emergence of new criminal groups (Pomiankiewicz 2006),
- corrupting officers or civilian employees of the Prison Service.

The Prison Service attaches the great importance to proper identification of the environment of inmates who are associated with organized criminal groups (Pomiankiewicz 2009). However, it does not have the means to deepen the obtained information, which leaves a wide scope for actions of law enforcement agencies.

## Perception of Prison Informers – Historical Aspect

In these deliberations an issue of negative perception of prison informers cannot be ignored. In Poland, in the years 1919 – 1939 objections to the use of secret collaborators gaining information from detainees in police custodies were raised (Netczuk 2006). They were introduced into a criminal proceeding in the form of testimonies submitted by informers on overt court hearings (Łukomski 1924). Therefore, it is difficult to understand what the actual cause of controversy was. Perhaps such actions may have been ethically dubious and on the verge of deception, but it is difficult to treat them as illegal.

The concept of prison informers completely changed in 1944 when, through extensive structure of secret collaborators of the security apparatus, communistic authorities tried to control every aspect of a social life in the country. At this time an extensive network of personal sources of information was established and deployed in detention centers and prisons. Prison informers played a very negative role in combating Polish independence underground in the years 1944 – 1956. Its presentation, however, is necessary as it will bring out fundamental differences in relation to the present status quo. Despite the lack of one definition it is assumed that the informer was a secret prison collaborator, recruited in a place of isolation such as a detention center, prison or labor camp, who was one of the inmates and who watched them. This group of informers was extremely highly rated by officers of the Security Offices and labelled as "serious investigative arms". It was created on the basis of Soviet designs, in particular the so called "podsiadki" (the informers deliberately placed in a cell).Their recruitment was conducted, among other things, by officers of special departments or by officers of the Security Offices (Czołgoszewski 2007). Also, chiefs of prisons could build their own network of personal sources of information but the majority of them neglected this opportunity. The condition of a prison informer's recruitment was a person's previous admission of guilt and so-called sincerity during the investigation and trial. An encouraging element to start cooperation was the possibility of improving an inmate's own living conditions (parcels, extra rations, walks, visits), promises of mitigation or reduction in sentence but sometimes physical force was used such as detention, beating, confinement to make prisoners cooperate. Also, who had been sentenced to death were recruited in exchange for possible judicial pardon. There were also cases of sentencing such informers to death penalty when the efficient conduct of the case was required, or if the agent himself occurred to be useless. Yet, some prison informers sentenced to death were pardoned and their previous sentence was changed into life imprisonment. It depended on their so-called further operational usefulness. In addition, a candidate for an informer had to have adequate mental and intellectual abilities such as: the ability to initiate contacts with other people and chat with them and ability to quick adaptation to new conditions. There was a ban on revealing prison informers the trial materials connected with the case they were involved in. To protect the prison informer against the possibility of being disclosed some strict rules of the use of information from denunciation during questioning were employed. Informers' working time was limited mostly to maximum one year. Prison informers like the other categories of personal sources of information were permanently controlled in terms of their credibility. One of such methods was putting in a cell two informers who knew nothing about each other's presence. Disclosing one of them meant immediate withdrawal of such an informer from the system and his temporary isolation from other prisoners. Nevertheless, there were some possibilities of the further use of the disclosed source of information for operational purposes, for example to strengthen a position of another prison informer. Also, the possibility of transferring an informer to another detention center or prison was taken into account. The primary purpose of their activities was to gain trust of "colleagues" from the cell and even befriend with them. This was to serve the detection of new offences undisclosed by an investigation and court and to prevent from establishing conspiracy in prison, with the view to the call to riots and escapes. Often as a result of prison informers' reports there were some cases of sentencing people to capital punishment and executing them. These informers also reported on the prison service workers. Depending on a range of tasks performed personal sources of information located in prisons and detection centers were divided into several categories – agents, informers and the group of so-called "loose contacts". In certain specific cases informers were given the task of carrying out a specific psychological game with other inmates the aim of which was to get them to confirm the criminal charges brought against them. This concerned the acts they had committed as well as the ones they had had no connection with. It was needed to officers of the Security Offices to fulfil statistical requirements imposed on them by the communist authorities and to demonstrate their effectiveness in operational work. After serving the sentence and being released, part of prison informers continued their cooperation with the secret police as personal sources of information (Wołoszyn 2010). Taking over the penitentiary system by the Ministry of Justice, as a result of political changes in Poland which took place in 1956, did not contribute to elimination of informers (Dominiczak 1997). Until the very end of Polish People's Republic, so until 1989, the prisoners who were perceived as a threat to the existing political system were still under intensive surveillance. It concerned, first of all, the activists of the Independent Self-Governing Trade Union 'Solidarity'. The preventative and criminal objectives did not matter in this case. All this meant that conducting the operational work by the Prison Service was officially banned by the Minister of Justice in the Ordinance No 17/1989/CZZK on November 21 1989. In turn, the Security Service, which played a major role in the management of prison informers, after democratic changes in Poland was transformed into the State Protection Office in 1990.

## THE CURRENT SITUATION

In Poland there are not currently any regulations or scientific studies relating to the way of functioning of prison informers. All the information is merely the verbal instructions for young policemen made by the more experienced ones. It should be noted that, in contrast to the situation that took place before 1989, there are numerous legal restrictions and the most important seems the one concerning the ban on recruitment of all categories of personal sources of information on the basis of incriminating materials possessed by a particular service. These deliberations will focus on operational and reconnaissance actions carried out primarily by the police due to the fact that their actions are mostly concentrated on the detection of criminal offences and prosecuting perpetrators, whilst the rules of operational and reconnaissance actions concerning internal and external security of the state are completely different and this is why they will not be a subject of this article.

The political changes that have taken place in Poland over the past twenty five years have caused very serious problems connected with the use of help of personal sources of information (Hanausek 2001). Some new, non-existing earlier problems have appeared concerning amongst other things:

- the use of incriminating materials during recruitment,
- the disclosure of professional or state secrecy when allocating tasks,
- the possession of objects, by informers performing tasks, that might indicate a crime such as drugs, weapons, counterfeit banknotes and documents,
- the so-called participating informer and the so-called controlled purchase (Rau 2009).

These problems were to be solved by the act on operational and reconnaissance actions (Projek ustawy 2008). However, the elapse of time since the submission of the draft in the Parliament and a lot of problems in the course of work on it, do not inspire particular optimism regarding an early entry the provisions contained therein. The numerous inconsistencies in the draft and interpretation doubts are caused by an attempt to find common rules for criminal service and also for civil and military special services (Netczuk 2010). It can cause a problem to accept the solutions proposed in the draft

(Tomaszewski 2010; Mąka 2009; Netczuk 2011). The lack of legal regulations of operational and reconnaissance actions in Poland is even more surprising that this sphere has been regulated in such countries as Russia, Ukraine or Belarus.

Based on a thorough analysis of the rules of operational actions, four situations can be mentioned when the police can initiate obtaining information from prison informers:

- the deliberate engagement of an informer staying outside prison by using validation documents,
- the use of an informer who was cooperated with outside the prison and who, after being arrested due to his criminal activity, was taken to the detention center,
- initiating a personal contact with the police by a candidate for a future prison informer during his stay in a penitentiary unit,
- the deliberate recruitment of a personal source of information to cooperate with the police during his stay in a police custody or prison.

The latter of the indicated ways is potentially the most effective because the recruitment to cooperate of the person having contacts with the members of the criminal group being under observation is the fastest way to gain access to it. The recruitment of such an informer does not require creating his false dossier, preparing validation documents so he can start the cooperation immediately. Thanks to the knowledge of structures of criminal groups and their hierarchy, effective disintegration and disinformation actions can be implemented. In the situation when a person is from outside their structures, it is always necessary to take into account that the lack of knowledge of the habits existing in such groups can lead to the quick disclosure of this person (Netczuk, 2006). It is particularly important in prison.

Determining motives which makes the recruitment easier requires not only a professional preparation of a police officer, but also the knowledge of a criminal environment. Universally applicable systems of values may differ significantly from the systems of values of detainees. It has been rightly pointed out that it is just inappropriate mental preparation of police officers which results most often in denying cooperation and disclosing the knowledge possessed by the police. Sometimes the above mentioned issues are additionally influenced by insufficient qualifications of a police officer and also illegal attempts to recruit a prison informer on the basis of an incriminating material (Horosiewicz 2012).

Nevertheless, penitentiary institutions provide an opportunity to use a rare motive to recruit personal sources of information. It is, amongst other things, actual or false conviction of a candidate for the personal source of information that the prisoner under observation is the threat to him. Creating such a motive requires skillful manipulation of information and the use of favorable circumstances, for example, the emergence of a situation that could lead to a conflict between the candidate for the prison informer and the person under observation. There is the necessity of creating the full control over the candidate for a source of information which is easier during his stay in a police custody or prison. Skillful disinformation and preventing the contact with the person under observation are aimed at maintaining the real or false conflict caused by an operational combination. The isolated, relevantly selected and dispensed information will form the conviction in the consciousness of a candidate for a prison informer, that the only way to eliminate the threat is to agree to cooperate with law enforcement institutions (Horosiewicz 2012).

Another motive which can make the recruitment of such a source of information easier is, for example, their disappointment concerning their own crime group. It happens for instance, when neither the candidate for the informer nor his family is helped by his partners. Then, such assistance, both material and non-material, can be offered by the police.

Among the motives that might prevent the recruitment of a source of information in a police custody or in prison can be, amongst other things, fear for losing their sources of income obtained through a cooperation with a criminal group, negative attitude towards the police as well as unknown affiliation with a person being under surveillance (Horosiewicz 2012).

The example of the badly prepared recruitment of a candidate for a prison informer is, for instance, a safe way to establish contact with him and bringing him to the first meeting. The lack of knowledge of the penitentiary unit customs means that a further action will be unsuccessful. For example, the Prison Service officers bring the function prisoner for the meeting with the chief responsible for the security of this unit using a different way than the inmate who is going to a visit room or who is going to take part in procedural actions. Ignoring this difference can cause that the candidate for a personal source of information can be revealed and, being afraid of his life or health, he will refuse to cooperate. Also, he can be disclosed before the beginning of the cooperation becoming useless in the future (Horosiewicz 2012).

A separate issue that needs to be considered is the use of prison informers as witnesses in a criminal trial. It is very rare in practice, since disclosing the personal source of information who was earlier successfully placed in the criminal group means the loss, often irretrievable, of the possibility of its surveillance. Therefore, before such a decision it must be considered if it is more useful to leave the informer in the criminal group and to use other sources of evidence in the criminal trial (Taracha 2006). It seems that, in the case of the above mentioned category of informers, extreme caution must be kept in this regard.

Defining prospects of the use of prison informers in operational and reconnaissance actions requires a presentation of an outline of the problems arising in the current practice of cooperation with personal sources of information (Herbowski 2014a; Herbowski 2014b). They are varied and virtually unknown outside the police community. They stem largely from the fact that, unlike the situation which took place in Poland before 1989, there is noticeable reluctance to initiate the cooperation as police informers in the fear of being disclosed. It is mainly caused by the fact that, a former and superior principle of protection of sources of information, is no longer used. Nowadays, there is a prevailing willingness to arrest the perpetrators identified by informers as soon as possible even if it could threaten their disclosure and, as a result, endanger their lives and health (Netczuk 2006). In addition, the recruitment of informers is largely focused on meeting the statistical requirements. Police officers must find a lot of sources and information the number of which affects their professional evaluation. The most appreciated informers are those who have a 'potential' access to a wide range of groups. In the actual practice some of such sources can be so-called "dead souls" (Ogdowski 2004; Herbowski 2014a). It is caused, amongst other things, by the lack of systematic and thorough control of actions of operational officers by their direct superiors (Horosiewicz 2014) and their incompetence. This creates the superiors' false belief that the number of secret collaborators in criminal circles is sufficient (Herbowski 2014a). It is not noticed that a formal position of a source in the hierarchy of personal sources of information (Gruza, Goc and Moszczyński 2008) does not mean that the reported information is valuable, and unfortunately, this is the way of thinking of many police decision-makers. Therefore, it is advisable to link the category of the source with the category of the unit as it determines in a crucial way the possibility of his management. It is difficult to imagine the cooperation with prison informers conducted by the police officers from their police station. It seems that due to the importance of the reported information and, above all, the specific difficulties in handling the process, it should be dealt with by the operational officers from operational departments of the Provincial Police Headquarters and The Central Bureau of Investigation.

The problems concerning the cooperation of the police officers with personal sources of information also result from the lack of a theoretical preparation of the police officers. The direct effect of such a situation is in many cases their awkwardness in recruiting informers. It often collides with unrealistic expectations of their superiors which was confirmed in the results of research conducted amongst operational police officers (Rau 2007).

The cooperation with secret collaborators is also made difficult by the fundamental generation change in the police forces. A visible effect of this is the fact that the young officers have nobody to be taught by (Rau 2013) and this is just experience which plays a crucial role in the work of the police officer especially in the situation when his training process takes many years. Frequent personnel changes in the police forces (Pytlakowski 2012) including the executives from criminal divisions cause that the supervision of the cooperation with informers is often apparent or even conservative (Horosiewicz 2013). Also, in many cases, officers are not properly instructed by their superiors as for such a cooperation. This is confirmed by the results of ministerial controls in which it has repeatedly been pointed out the wrong interpretation, poor knowledge or even ignorance of the rules of operational work (Zarządzenie 2006, 2008, 2011) amongst those responsible for both functional and instance official supervision. It seems that the system of checking and controlling the work of informers which has been perfected for many years, just fails (Horosiewicz 2013). Their controls are mostly formal. What is more, the comprehensive development of the source of information is not required, which is especially important in the case of prison informers.

## Conclusion

The police have always kept criminal circles under surveillance placing inside them their informers. Without such actions, gaining success in the fight against crime particularly the organized one is impossible. In Poland, however, there is the necessity of significant changes in the methods of obtaining information by law enforcement agencies especially as far as personal sources of information are concerned. Facing the current forms and dynamics of organized crime, the ban on the use of prison informers would be completely irrational. Even if this category personal sources of information is not regulated by legislature, it will not disappear, like some politicians thought in 1989. Currently, however, there is a different field of prison informers' interest. Information obtained by them can be very useful in an effort to combat criminality, in particular organized crime. Contrary to the fears, this information is not used to fight with the political opposition or it does not interfere with the correctional process of prisoners.

These days, however, there are much more difficult conditions for the recruitment and cooperation with prison informers. They stem directly from numerous problems arising in the course of the police cooperation with 'common' personal sources of information. To make this method of operational work effective, the good organization, precise control and detailed analysis of the tasks assigned to the people are required. Unfortunately, in this area it is visible the necessity of introducing numerous and thoroughly considered changes. It must be agreed that, contrary to the actual needs, there are currently no prospects for wider use of prison informers in operational and reconnaissance actions.

## References


Bulsiewicz, A. (1992). The role of a trusted person in operational and reconnaissance activities and the criminal proceedings. *Przegląd Policyjny*, 2-3, 25-33.

Bulsiewicz, A. (1997). The issue of a trusted person in current legislation and proposed amendments in Poland. In H.J. Hirsch, P. Hofmański, E. Pływaczewski, & C. Roxin (Eds.), *The criminal law and the criminal proceeding in the face of the new forms and techniques of crime* (pp. 457-467). Białystok: Temida 2.

Cempura, A. (2011). Operational reconnaissance conducted in detention wards and penal institutions. *Prokuratura i Prawo*, 10, 123-133.

Cenckiewicz, S. (2011). *The long arm of Moscow. Military Intelligence in Polish People's Republic 1943-1991 (introduction to synthesis).* Poznań: Zysk i S-ka.

Czołgoszewski, J. (2007). Historical background of operational work in Polish prisons in the years 1945-1956. In T. Bulenda, W. Knap, & Z. Lasocik (Eds.), *The penitentiary system at the beginning of the twenty-first century. III Polish Penitentiary Congress* (pp. 305-314). Warszawa: IPSIR UW.

Dominiczak, H. (1997). *Security authorities of PRL 1944-1990: the development and activity in the light of documents of MSW.* Warszawa: Bellona.

Gruza E., Goc M., & Moszczyński J. (2008). *Criminalistics – the thing about investigative methods.* Warszawa: Wydawnictwa Akademickie i Profesjonalne.

Hanausek, T. (2001). Criminalistics in Poland at the turn of centuries. *Problemy Kryminalistyki*, 232, 5-8.

Herbowski, P. (2014a). Some problems of cooperation of police officers with informants. *Nowa Kodyfikacja Prawa Karnego*, *XXXIV*, 119-133.

Herbowski, P. (2014b). The Problem of Proper Supervision of Superiors over Remunerating Personal Sources of Information. *Security Dimensions International & National Studies*, *12*, 69-75.

Horosiewicz, K. (2013).Superiors' Supervision over Cooperation of Police Officers with Covert Human Information. *Przegląd Policyjny*, 3, 241-250.

Horosiewicz, K. (2012). Recruitment Undertakings. *Przegląd Policyjny*, 4, 210-220.

Information (2008) on the results of operations of the Central Anti-Corruption Bureau in 2008. http://cba.gov.pl/ftp/filmy/Informacja_o_wynikach_dzialalnosci_Centralnego_Biura_Antykorupcyjnego_w_2008_roku.pdf.

Jabrzyk, J. (2013). "The reversed" the former agents of CBA. They work for a criminal in the a company illegally disposing waste. http://www.tvn24.pl/wiadomosci-z-kraju,3/odwroceni-byli-agenci-cba-pracuja-dla-kryminalisty-w-firmie-nielegalnie-utylizujacej-odpady,330588.html.

Kolejwa, M. (1984). Confidential personal sources of information in criminalistics research. In M. Kolejwa, (Ed.), *Confidential personal sources of information in reconnaissance, surveillance and detection of perpetrators of criminal offences. Materials from the scientific conference in Warsaw 26-27 September 1983,* (pp. 26-44). Warszawa: Instytut Kryminalistyki Akademii Spraw Wewnętrznych.

Łukomski, B. (1924). *Investigation service and criminal tactics with the most important news from forensic medicine, for the use of the Police, police schools and investigative judges: based on the works.* Lwów: Księgarnia Maksymiljana Bodeka.

Mąka, J. (2009). Law on Operational Reconnaissance – is it needed in the current legal regime governing in Poland? *Prokuratura i Prawo*, *4*, 126-151.

Mirfield, P. (1997). *Silence, Confessions and Improperly Obtained Evidence.* Oxford: Oxford University Press.

Musiał, F. (2013). Typing, developing, recruiting and work with secret collaborators. Two analyses by Stanisław Wałach in the years 1972-1974.

In F. Musiał (Ed.), *Personal measures of operational work – the issues of sources* (pp. 397-425). Kraków: Wydawnictwo Dante.

Netczuk, R. (2001). Undercover policeman in the light of the new criminal proceedings code and the Police Act. *Problemy Prawa Karnego, 24,* 126-143.

Netczuk, R. (2006). *Secret collaborator of the Police in the face of comparative law.* Katowice: Wydawnictwo Uniwersytetu Śląskiego.

Netczuk, R. (2010). Secret collaborator and secret agent in the projects of the act concerning operational and reconnaissance work: remarks de lege ferenda. *Wojskowy Przegląd Prawniczy, 3,* 11-30.

Netczuk, R. (2011). Operational law – the beginning of new hope or the revenge of the Siths? *Przegląd Policyjny 2011, 3,* 81-104.

Ogdowski, M. (2004). Cops and informers. http://www.przeglad-tygodnik.pl/pl/artykul/gliniarze-uchole

Pismo Dyrektora Generalnego Służby Więziennej nr ZDP 00-50/06 z dnia 29 marca 2006 r., unpublished.

Pomiankiewicz, J. (2006). The penitentiary system in the face of the problem of operational work. *Prokurator*, 4, 46-50.

Pomiankiewicz, J. (2009). Members of organized criminal groups in remand centers and penitentiaries – threats to the Prison Service and the counteractions taken. In L. Paprzycki, & Z. Rau (Eds.), *Practical elements of the fight against organized crime and terrorism. Modern technologies and operational work* (pp. 695-711). Warszawa: Wolters Kluwer.

The project of the Act (2008) on operational and reconnaissance work. www.orka.sejm.gov.pl/proc6.nsf/projekty/353_p.htm.

Pytlakowski, P. (2012). Great changes in the leadership of the Police. The police carousel. http://www.polityka.pl/tygodnikpolityka/kraj/1524223,1,wielkie-zmiany-w-kierownictwie-policji.read?backTo= http://www.polityka.pl/tygodnikpolityka/kraj/1587501,1,pozegnanie-policjanta-despero.read.

Rau, Z. (2007). The selected causes of corruption allegation towards police officers. In Z. Bielecki, & J. Szafrański (Eds.), *Combating corruption crime in Poland* (pp. 105-119). Szczytno: Wyższa Szkoła Policji.

Rau, Z. (2009). Operational reconnaissance activities in the Polish legal system – efforts to adopt a universal law. In L. Paprzycki, & Z. Rau (Eds.), Practical elements of the fight against organized crime and terrorism. Modern technologies and operational work (pp. 712-745). Warszawa: Wolters Kluwer.

Rau, Z. (2013). Interview for TV channel TVN in the program Czarno na białym emitted on 9.04.2013, http://www.tvn24.pl/wideo/z-anteny/ ryzykowna gra,724856.html?playlist_id=17209.

Taracha, A. (2006). *The operational and reconnaissance, criminalistics and legal aspects.* Lublin: Wydawnictwo Uniwersytetu Marii Curie-Skłodowskiej.

Tomaszewski, T. (2010). The project of the act on operational and reconnissance activities – the critical analysis. In E. Gruza, M. Goc, & T. Tomaszewski (Eds.), *What is new in criminalistics – the review of issues on combating crime* (pp. 347-356). Warszawa: Stowarzyszenie Absolwentów Wydziału Prawa i Administracji UW.

Ustawa o Policji (The Police Act) (1990) - uniform text. Laws of 2011. No. 287, item. 1687, as amended. d.

Wołoszyn, J. (2010). "Sharp weapon – prison agents. Secret collaborators in penitentiaries and dentention centers in the years 1944-1956. *Pamięć i Sprawiedliwość. Pismo Instytutu Pamięci Narodowej*, 2, 295-319.

Young-sook Kim, K. (1991). Self-incrimination, compulsion and the undercover agents – Illinois v. Perkins, 110. S. Ct. 2394 (1990). *Washington Law Review*, *66*, 605-622.

Zarządzenie (Ordinance No. PF -634 KGP dated 30.06.2006). On the methods and forms of exercise by the police operational and reconnaissance activities, unpublished; Ordinance No. PF - 1292-1208 KGP dated 19.12.2008. Amending the Ordinance on the methods and forms of exercise by the police operational and reconnaissance activities, unpublished; Ordinance No. PF - 671/11 dated 07.06.2011 KGP. Amending the Ordinance on the methods and forms of exercise by the police operational and reconnaissance activities, unpublished.

In: Law Enforcement and Crime
Editor: Emanuel T. Rhodes

ISBN: 978-1-63484-127-6


*Chapter 5*

# VISUALIZATION OF HOMICIDE RATES IN THE US AND CORRELATIONS WITH OTHER GEOSTATISTIC DATA PROVIDED BY DENSITY-EQUALIZING MAPS

***Karina I. Mazzitello*[*] *and Julián Candia*[†]**
Instituto de Investigaciones Científicas
y Tecnológicas en Electrónica,
CONICET-UNMdP, Mar del Plata, Argentina
Department of Physics,
University of Maryland, College Park, MD, US

**Abstract**

In general, the collection of statistical data at local, regional or national level requires extensive funding that is provided by different organizations. These data are collected in large tables and used for different purposes by many entities. It is difficult to relate data by simple inspection of the tables. Consequently, it is worth representing these data on elegant maps that are useful and easily readable. The visualization method used for the construction of these maps is based on ideas from elementary physics. The regular map regions are rescaled to be proportional to statistical values of each region, so the statistical density on the rescaled

[*]E-mail address: kmazzite@mdp.edu.ar
[†]E-mail address: juliancandia@gmail.com

map is homogeneously distributed. The method allows one to choose a balance between good density equalization and low distortion of map regions. We study the homicide rates in the U.S. and their correlation with other publicly available data applying this nonstandard visualization technique. Finally, a comparison of homicide rates in the U.S. to that of different Latin American countries is shown.

# 1. Introduction

The increasing proliferation of a broad array of geographically referenced data derived from different sources enables a deep analysis of social behaviors that trigger and stimulate interdisciplinary efforts involving a wide variety of academic disciplines. Methods to analyze statistical data based on multilevel Voronoi tessellation [1] and multilayered complex network analysis and modeling [2, 3] offer promising avenues of research. Geography and statistics are ubiquitously intertwined in data collected to assess the levels of health, socioeconomic development, literacy and education, crime, and many other key indicators of the welfare of society. However, georeferenced data are most often represented by traditional visualization methods such as bar and pie charts, regression plots, box plots and standard maps with color codes by region, which do a poor job in integrating these two key aspects. This chapter deals with the implementation of a physics-based visualization approach to integrating geography and statistics into a unified framework. Some examples of new visualization techniques recently developed are state-of-the-art animations to see the quantum world, accurate maps of the universe based on the Sloan Digital Sky Survey covering large areas of the sky, and complex network representations that facilitate the recognition of patterns in multidimensional complex systems [4, 5, 6].

Recent research based on ideas from physics has focused on creating the so-called cartograms, in which geographic regions are deformed and rescaled in proportion to their population or other statistical indicators. For instance, the methods proposed by Appel et al. [7] and by Dorling [8] are based on cellular automata, in which local interaction rules allow boundaries to shrink or expand locally until equilibrium is reached. In the approach by Gusein-Zade and Tikunov [9], a continuous displacement field is used to expand high population areas by means of a repulsive force. Another procedure proposed by Kocmoud [10] relies on a mechanical model of masses and springs, which is constrained in order to maintain certain topographic features. Despite these efforts, cartograms built following those methods proved to be problematic in a number of ways, leading to highly distorted shapes, overlapping regions, or strong dependences on the choice of coordinate axes.

More recently, Gastner and Newman [11] proposed a new method for building cartograms based on diffusion equations, which resolves the shortcomings experienced with previous techniques. Starting with an inhomogeneously distributed statistical quantity (e.g., the population density), diffusion equations are numerically integrated with appropriate boundary conditions. By allowing the diffusion process to evolve until a homogeneous equilibrium state is reached, the displacements can be reinterpreted to generate a cartogram.

Within this context, in this chapter, we implement the diffusion-based method to create a variety of density- equalizing maps of the U.S. With this approach we generate a series of cartograms that show different ways of displaying homicide rates. Depending on the way the cartograms are built and how the statistics are chosen, different perspectives can be gained from the data. Also, cross-correlations between homicide rates and other statistical quantities are represented proving to be a more effective way than the standard visual methods previously mentioned.

This chapter is structured as follows. Section 2 is devoted to explaining the diffusion-based cartogram method. In Subsection 3.1, we give a brief discussion of the method comparing diffusion cartograms with maps with color codes. In Subsection 3.2, we analyze the correlations between the homicide rates of the U.S and other demographic variables. Local and global distortions of the U.S map with different levels of coarse-graining for the homicide rates are presented in Subsection 3.3. The concluding remarks are finally stated in Section 4.

## 2. The Diffusion-Based Cartogram Method

The diffusion-based method for generating density-equalizing maps relies on Fick's first law, in which it is postulated that the flux of a solute goes from regions of high concentration to regions of low concentration, in the absence of an external field. If these regions have impermeable and mobile boundaries, the solute will move the boundaries due to pressure difference until the quantity of solute is uniform within each region. Thus, one way to create a cartogram, given a particular density of a statistical indicator that we want to represent, is to allow the movement of all region boundaries on the map until the density is equalized everywhere, as occurs for a solute according to Fick's first law. The statistical indicator, distributed inhomogeneously in the different regions of a map, can be the population, the homicide rate, the vote in an election, the cases of a certain disease, etc.

Let us consider $\rho_0(\vec{r})$, the spatial density distribution of the inhomogeneous statistical indicator to be represented by means of a rescaled map. If the total area of the map is preserved, the homogeneous density of the statistical indicator after rescaling will be equal to the mean density before rescaling, $\langle\rho_0\rangle$. From a mathematical point of view, any total-area- preserving map rescaling operation corresponds to a coordinate transformation $\vec{r} \to \vec{r}'$ under the condition that the determinant of the corresponding Jacobian matrix equal the density ratio $\rho_0\left(\vec{r}\right) / \langle\rho_0\rangle$. Although this condition guarantees that the total area of the map remains constant, it does not provide specific information about the cartogram projection. In order to determine a unique projection, we resort to the physical process of diffusion by considering the spatial density as a time-dependent scalar field, $\rho\left(\vec{r}, t\right)$, that satisfies the initial condition $\rho\left(\vec{r}, t = 0\right) \equiv \rho_0\left(\vec{r}\right)$. From a macroscopic perspective, the current density, related to time-dependent velocity and density fields through

$$\vec{J} = \rho\left(\vec{r}, t\right)\vec{v}\left(\vec{r}, t\right) \ , \tag{1}$$

is directed along the gradient of the density field

$$\vec{J} = D\vec{\nabla}\rho \ , \tag{2}$$

where the minus sign implies that the flow is always directed from regions of high density to regions of low density and will be faster when the gradient is steeper. We set, in Eq. (2) without loss of generality, $D = 1$, conveniently choosing time and length units. These equations, together with the equation for the local conservation of mass,

$$\vec{\nabla} \cdot J + \frac{\partial \rho}{\partial t} = 0 \ , \tag{3}$$

lead to the well-known diffusion equation

$$\nabla^2 \rho - \frac{\partial \rho}{\partial t} = 0 \ . \tag{4}$$

We enclose the map within a huge box (two to three times the linear extent of the area to be mapped is enough), whose initial density is uniform and it matches the mean density $\langle \rho_0 \rangle$ of the statistical indicator to be represented in the cartogram. The role of this box is to keep the total area of the map constant during the diffusion process. We choose Neumann boundary conditions on the walls of the box, in which no flow of the statistical variable occurs through them. Thus, the calculation of the cartogram involves solving the diffusion equation for $\rho(\vec{r}, t)$ (Eq. 4), with the initial condition $\rho(\vec{r}, t = 0) \equiv \rho_0(\vec{r})$ and the Neumann boundary condition. Then, the velocity field is calculated as

$$\vec{v}(\vec{r}, t) = \frac{\vec{\nabla}\rho}{\rho} \tag{5}$$

and from the latter, the cumulative displacement of any point on the map can be calculated by solving the kinematics, i.e.,

$$\vec{r}(t) = \vec{r}(0) + \int_0^t \vec{r}(t) \ . \tag{6}$$

In the large-t limit the set of such displacements for all points on the original map defines the cartogram.

These considerations basically specify the diffusion-based cartogram method (see [11] for more details of its actual implementation).

# 3. Results and Discussion

## 3.1. Density-Equalizing Cartograms Versus Standard Maps of the U.S.

This section relates to the implementation of the diffusion-based method to generate density-equalizing cartograms of the contiguous U.S. states. The term contiguous excludes the non-contiguous states of Alaska and Hawaii and all offshore United States territories and possessions, which include American Samoa, Guam, the Northern Mariana Islands, Puerto Rico, and the United States Virgin Islands. We examined the murder and nonnegligent manslaughter rates by state using data from the Federal Bureau of Investigation (FBI), whose last report was made in 2013 [12]. In the FBI's Uniform Crime Reporting (UCR)

Program, murder and nonnegligent manslaughter is defined as the willful (nonnegligent) killing of one human being by another. It is distinguished from involuntary manslaughter by the presence of intention. This classification of offense, hereinafter referred to as homicides in this chapter, is based solely on police investigation as opposed to the determination of a court, medical examiner, coroner, jury, or any other judicial body. The UCR Program does not include the following situations in this offense classification: deaths caused by negligence, suicide, or accident; justifiable homicides; and attempts to murder or assaults to murder, which are classified as aggravated assaults in that program.

First, we represent the homicide rates per 100.000 inhabitants on a standard map of the U.S. (Figure 1(a)). Washington D. C, is included in Maryland (MD), increasing its rate from 6.4 to 7.4. Roughly, there is a polarization of the homicide rates between the northern and southern regions of the U.S. This is clearly observed in Figure 1(a), in which the homicide rates for each state are shown by means of grayscale shading: darker states have higher murder rates, while lighter states have lower ones. This color-coded map, in which the shapes and areas of the states are faithful geographical representations, is very usual. Accurate geographical information comes at a price: states like Maryland (MD) and Louisiana (LA) with high homicide rates appear barely noticeable due to their small surface areas. Moreover, although the preferential focus of attention (size, shape, or color) might depend on the subject, standing out on this map are the states with large surface areas, which might not be relevant neither by having particularly high homicide rates. A good example in this regard is offered by two of the larger states, Texas (TX) and Montana (MT), which rank 22nd and 41st among the 48 contiguous states in the list of states with highest homicide rates (using statistics corresponding to 2013 [12]).

In order to put in evidence the states with higher homicide rates, we generate the cartogram of Figure 1(b) by assuming $\rho_0(\vec{r}) = (\text{Homicide Rate})_i / A_i$, for all $\vec{r}$ belonging to the area of the $i$th state, $A_i$. The density-equalizing diffusion-based method thus leads to a representation in which the area of each state is in proportion to its homicide rate. The states as Louisiana (LA) and Maryland (MD) (including Washington DC) stand out with respect to Montana (MT), thus emphasizing the big difference in their homicide rates.

Note that we kept the same grayscale shading on both figures (Figures 1(a) and (b)); however, the grayscales in the cartogram can be used to represent other demographic variables. Naturally, the cartogram approach trades off geographical accuracy in exchange for emphasizing a given statistical variable and

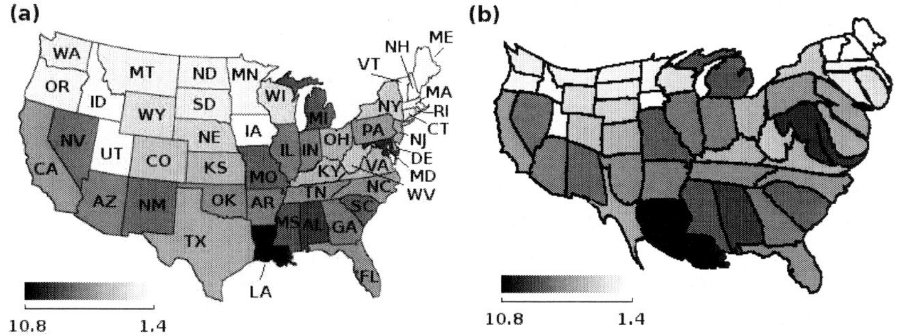


Figure 1. Comparison between (a) an unchanged map of the U.S. with color-coded homicide rates per 100000 inhabitants in 2013, for each state labeled by means of their abbreviations and (b) a cartogram showing the state areas proportional to their homicide rates. In both, darker regions have higher homicide rates while lighter regions have lower ones. The highest homicide rate is 10.8 (Louisiana (LA), in black) and the lowest one is 1.4 (Iowa (IA), in white). In cartogram (b), the states like Louisiana (LA) and Maryland (MD) including Washington DC stand out with respect to Montana (MT), due to the big difference between their area sizes.

incorporating additional information by means of different shadings, as we shall see in the next section.

### 3.2. Correlations between Homicide Rates and Other Demographic Variables

Uncovering correlations between crime statistics and other demographic, social, and economic variables is an active focus of research aiming at understanding the conditions that foster criminal behavior. For instance, Gould et al. found that low wages and unemployment make less-educated men more likely to turn to crime [13]. The impact of unemployment on crime has also been studied very recently using country-level statistical data from Europe [14]. Other recent studies on crime-rate regressions are reported, e.g., in Refs. [15, 16, 17] and references therein. Following our case study of state level homicide rates in the U.S., let us now analyze how correlations can be put in evidence by using diffusion- based cartograms. A similar study was done in [20], in which this

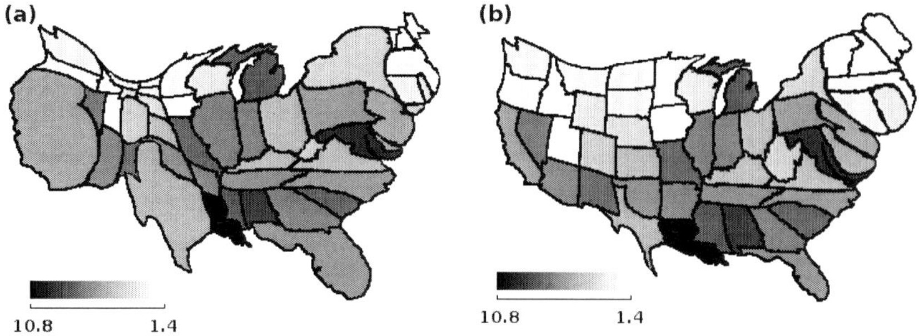


Figure 2. Comparison between two cartograms showing the state areas proportional to (a) their populations and (b) the logarithm of their populations. In both, the grayscale shading shows each state's homicide rates per 100,000 inhabitants in 2013. The second cartogram is more similar to that shown in Fig. 1(b) as there is a weak correlation between homicide rates and the logarithm of population.

kind of cartogram was used to show the correlation between homicide rates in Brazil and the IFDM index (the IFDM index measures the combined education, health, and economic development at the municipal level based on official data released by the Brazilian Ministries of Education).

It is known that, the homicide count is notably higher in more populated regions and vice versa, whereas that the homicide rate does not follow this rule. We suspect that there is no linear correlation between homicide rate and population. This uncorrelation is observed in Figure 2(a), in which a population cartogram of the 2010 U.S is shown [18]. The area of each state is in proportion to its population and as in Figure 1(b), the grayscale shading shows each state's homicide rates per 100,000 inhabitants in 2013. The darker states are not the largest states, making evident the linear uncorrelation. In addition, cartogram 2(a) is very different from that discussed in the previous section, in which the areas are proportional to their homicide rates (see Figure 1(b)). To confirm the uncorrelation, we calculate Pearson's coefficient $r$, which is good for measuring the strength of the linear relationship between pairs of the statistics variables $X$, $Y$, defined as

$$r = \frac{cov\,(XY)}{\sigma_X \sigma_Y} \tag{7}$$

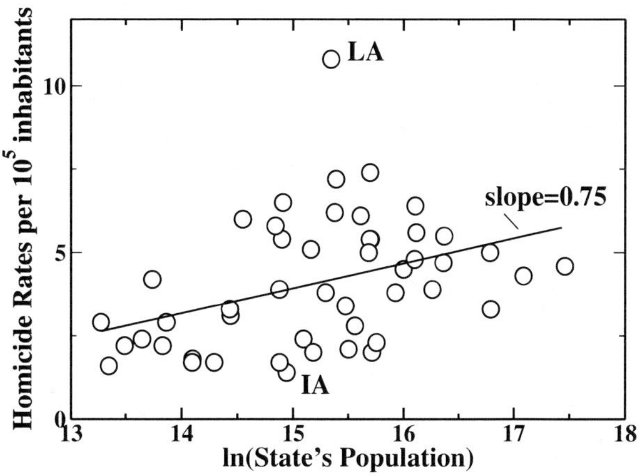


Figure 3. Scatterplot showing homicide rates per 100,000 inhabitants in 2013 and the logarithm of population by state (corresponding to the year 2010). The data corresponding to Louisiana (LA) and Iowa (IA) are labeled as references of the highest and the lowest homicide rates of the contiguous U.S. states, respectively. The solid line is the best linear fit to the data.

where, $cov$ is the covariance ($cov\,(X,Y) = \langle X - \langle X\rangle\rangle\,\langle Y - \langle Y\rangle\rangle$, $\langle ...\rangle$ means average value) and $\sigma$ is the standard deviation. The coefficient $r$ gives a value between $+1$ and $-1$, where $+1$ is total positive correlation, 0 is no correlation, and $-1$ is total negative correlation. In this case, the variables $X$ and $Y$ are the population and the homicide rate or vice versa. For these two statistics variables, $r = 0.19$ results.

To know whether the value obtained for $r$ has any sense, we performed a significance test using Student's t-distribution, not described here, on the coefficient and found that there is no evidence to suggest that there is a linear correlation between the homicide rate and population [19]. However, we found that the homicide rate is correlated with the logarithm of the population. Rather than the population by state, cartogram 2(b) shows the area of each state in proportion to the logarithm of its population, resulting more similar to cartogram 1(b). Indeed, the scatterplot in Figure 3 on both statistics is shown and the linear fit with slope $0.75$ hints to a possible correlation between them. In this case,

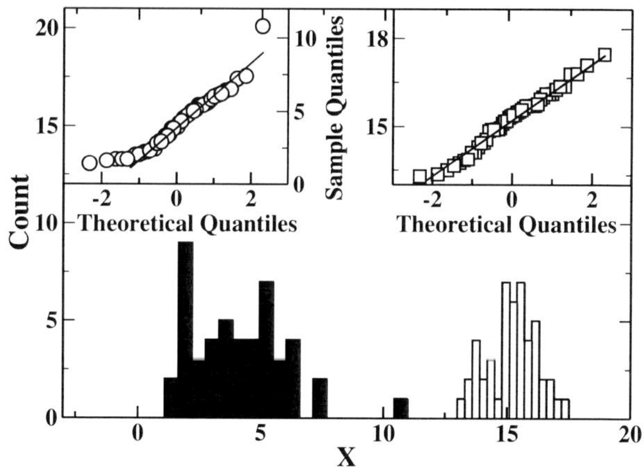


Figure 4. Histograms of homicide rates per 100,000 inhabitants in 2013 (hatched bars) and the logarithm of population by state corresponding to the year 2010 (open bars). $X$ represents the homicide rate for the first histogram and the logarithm of population for the second one. The insets show the normal Q-Q plots corresponding to each histogram: circle (square) symbols correspond to the histogram of homicide rates (logarithm of population). The histograms are almost normally distributed since the data of the insets are on or near the straight lines. The mean and the median are $(4.09, 3.90)$ for square symbols and $(15.23, 15.36)$ for circle symbols.

Pearson's correlation coefficient is equal to $0.37$, with a degree of confidence greater than $99\%$. This correlation value is weak as is shown in Figure 1(b), in which, for instance, the state areas of Alabama and Michigan are not large enough and however, they have high homicide rates compared to other states.

Pearson's correlation coefficient is sensitive to skewed distributions and outliers. Then, it is necessary to know whether the statistical distributions of the homicide rates and the logarithms of populations are skewed or normally distributed and there is indeed a weak correlation. In Figure 4, histograms of the homicide rates and the logarithms of the populations are shown. Bell shapes of normal distributions are difficult to verify graphically. Then, to check whether both histograms are individually normally distributed and thus confirm the correlation value $r = 0.37$, we plot Q-Q normal for each of them in the insets of Figure 4. Q-Q normal is a popular method (Q means quantil) to display data by plotting the quantiles of the values against the corresponding quantiles of the normal (bell shapes). The quantiles of the standard normal distribution are represented by a straight line. The normality of the data can be evaluated by observing the extent to which the points appear on the line. The insets of Figure 4 show that most of the data points associated with the histograms are on or near the straight lines, suggesting that the data are almost normally distributed in both histograms.

For a further testing of data normality, we can check the mean and median of each dataset. The mean is the average of the values, and the median is the second quartile. When the data are normally distributed around the mean, then the mean and median should be equal. Since the mean and the median $(4.09, 3.90)$ for the Q-Q plot of homicide rates are very close, the data (hatched bars in Figure 4), seem quite symmetric. The same analysis is valid for the Q-Q plot of the logarithms of populations (open bars in Figure 4) in which the mean and the median are $(15.23, 15.36)$.

Summing up, an analysis of the statistics distributions is needed when Pearson's coefficient evidences a plausible correlation between them. In the following, similar evaluations of the distributions are made and only the final results are shown.

Besides sustaining a weak linear correlation with the population's logarithm, the homicide rate is correlated with other demographic variables. We studied correlations with other violent crimes in the U.S., namely, rape, robbery and aggravated assault, reported by the FBI [12]. Violent crimes are defined in the UCR Program as those offenses that involve force or threat of force. Figure 5(a) shows scatterplots of the different violent crime rates versus homicide rates per 100,000 inhabitants in 2013. Rape and homicide rates are uncorrelated, since we found a Pearson's correlation coefficient equal to $0.04$ and a linear fit with a slope close to zero (see Figure 5(a)). Before proceeding further it can be mentioned that the rape rate is uncorrelated with any other violent crimes and also with the number of inhabitants. We studied the rape rates in metropolitan areas and nonmetropolitan counties by U.S. state and found a clear uncorrelation with the population. The analysis of these features is beyond the scope of the present work and therefore is not shown here.

Following with the study of correlations between violent crimes, a Pearson's coefficient equal to $0.62$, with a degree of confidence greater than $99\%$ is found

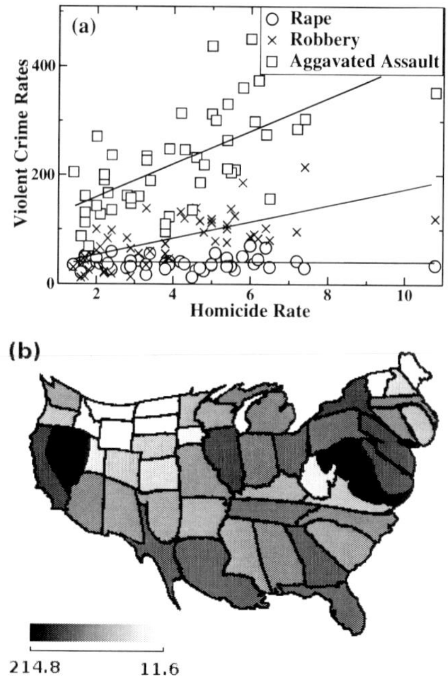


Figure 5. (a) Scatterplots showing homicide rates and different violent crime rates (the datasets are per 100,000 inhabitants and correspond to 2013). The solid lines are the best linear fits to each dataset. (b) Cartogram showing areas proportional to each state's homicide rates and the grayscale shading corresponding to each state's robbery rates (darker states have higher robbery rates). The highest robbery rate is 214.8 (Maryland (MD) plus Washington, DC in black) and the lowest one is 11.6 (Vermont (VT), in white).The cartogram puts in evidence the high correlation of robbery and homicide rates, for instance, the large, dark southern regions (indicating high crime rates) and, inversely, the comparatively smaller and lighter northeastern and northwestern states.

between the homicide rate and both, robbery and aggravated assault rates (see Figure 5(a)). As with the logarithm of population, we assessed whether robbery and aggravated assault rate data are normally distributed using the Q-Q plot method, thus confirming the strong correlation previously found.

From datasets shown in Figure 5(a), we chose to represent the correlation between robbery and homicide rates in a cartogram. Figure 5(b) shows this cartogram that, as in Figure 1(b), displays each state's area proportional to its homicide rate per 100,000 inhabitants in 2013. The grayscale shading represents each state's robbery rates (where darker states have higher robbery rates). The cartogram conveys correlations of robbery and homicide rates, for instance, the large, dark southern regions (indicating high crime rates) and, inversely, the comparatively smaller and lighter northeastern and northwestern states.

Different types of weapons are used in homicides, from firearms, knives or cutting instruments to hands, fists, feet, etc. In the FBI's Uniform Crime Reporting (UCR) Program, the murders are classified by type of weapons used. Figure 6(a) shows that the percentage of murders with firearms and the homicide rate reveal a plausible positive correlation. Indeed, a Pearson's coefficient equal to $0.65$, with a degree of confidence greater than 99% is found between these two statistics, assuming that the firearm dataset is normally distributed. Figure 6(b) is similar to cartogram 5(b), in which the state's areas are proportional to its homicide rates and the percentage of murders with firearms for each state are shown by means of grayscale shading: darker states have a higher percentage while lighter states have a lower one. The percentage of homicides with firearms is higher in states with higher homicide rates and vice versa. However, the existence of a strong correlation does not imply a causal link between the variables, but just means that both of them share information. To determine causes is a matter that cannot exclusively be resolved by mathematical tools, a deep knowledge of the subject is needed. This analysis is beyond the scope of this chapter.

Finally, in Figure 7(a) we show the relationship between the Human Development Index (HDI) and the homicide rates by state in 2013. The HDI index is a comparative measure of life expectancy, literacy, education, standards of living, and quality of life for countries worldwide. It is a standard means of measuring well-being, especially child welfare. It is used to distinguish whether the country is a developed, a developing or an underdeveloped country, and also to measure the impact of economic policies on the quality of life. Since the HDI index is a measure of welfare and prosperity, it is reasonable to expect states with higher HDI scores to be less affected by violent crimes and vice versa. Indeed, the scatterplot in Figure 7(a) hints to a correlation between the two statistics, as evidenced by a best linear fit with negative slope (shown by the solid line) and a Pearson's correlation coefficient equal to $-0.40$ and a degree of confidence

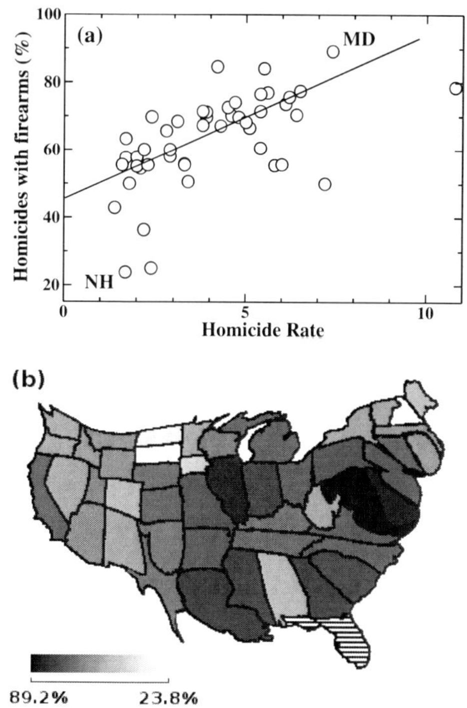


Figure 6. (a) Scatterplots showing homicide rates and percentages of homicides with firearms (both corresponding to 2013). The solid line is the best linear fit to the data. The data corresponding to Maryland (LA) and New Hampshire (NH) are labeled as references of the highest and the lowest percentages of homicides with firearms of the contiguous U.S. states, respectively. (b) Cartogram showing areas proportional to each state's homicide rates per 100,000 inhabitants in 2013 and the grayscale shading corresponding to each state's percentage of homicides with firearms (darker states have a higher percentage). The cartogram puts in evidence that states like Maryland (MD) plus Washington, DC and Mississippi (MS) have high percentages of homicides with firearms and also high homicide rates. The Florida state area is hatched since there are no available data on the percentage of homicides with firearms.

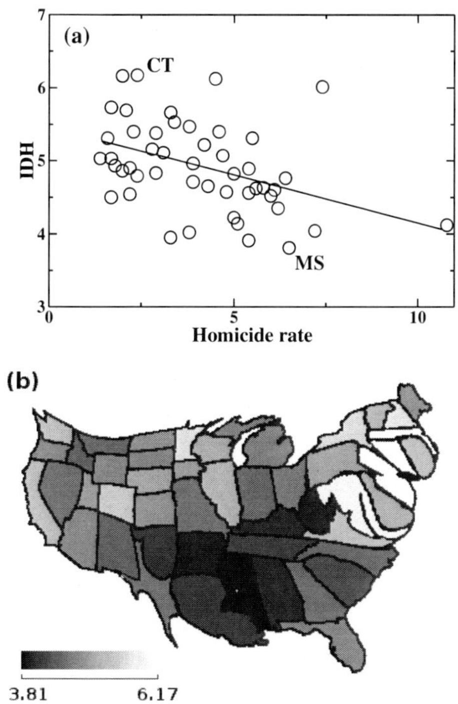


Figure 7. (a) Scatterplot showing homicide rates and the HDI index (corresponding to 2013 and 2010, respectively). The solid line is the best linear fit to the data. (b) Cartogram showing areas proportional to each state's homicide rates per 100,000 inhabitants in 2013 and the grayscale shading corresponding to each state's HDI index. Darker regions have less socioeconomic support at the municipal level, and these regions tend to have higher homicide rates. The highest index is 6.17 (Connecticut (CT), in white) and the lowest index is 3.81 (Mississippi (MS), in black).

greater than 99%, assuming that the index is normally distributed. Figure 7(b) shows a cartogram similar to cartograms 5(b) and 6, in which the state's areas are proportional to its homicide rates and the grayscale shading represents each state's HDI index (where darker states have lower HDI scores).

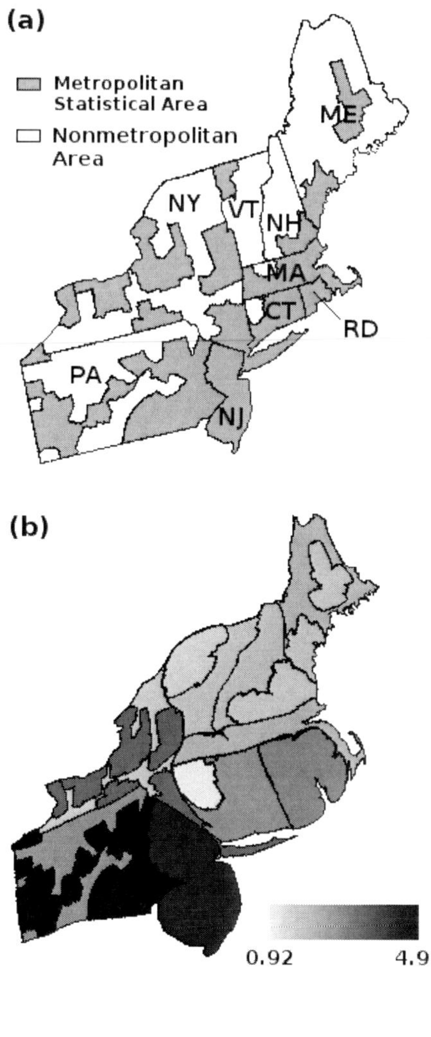


Figure 8. (a) Map of the northeast region of the U.S. metropolitan areas containing core urban areas of 50,000 or more population (gray areas in the map). (b) Cartogram of the northeastern region of the U.S. with a moderate coarse-graining showing areas proportional to each region's homicide rates per 100,000 inhabitants, divided into metropolitan and nonmetropolitan areas. Grayscale shading corresponds to each region's homicide rates. Darker and larger areas have higher homicide rates. For most of the states, the metropolitan areas are more dangerous.

Figure 9. Cartogram showing the change in areas (relative to their geographically faithful size) proportional to each country's homicide rates per 100,000 inhabitants with grayscale shading that reflects these same values at logarithmic scale. The data for Latin America were obtained from the United Nations Office on Drugs and Crime (UNODC) [21] (corresponding to the year 2012, except for Argentina and French Guiana data that correspond to 2010 and 2009, respectively). The homicide rate in the continental U.S. is 4.26 (year 2013). This value is low compared to Latin America's values. The continental U.S. shares the second rating as a safe country with Cuba followed by Argentina (with 5.2). The lowest homicide rate is 3.09 (Chile) whereas the highest one is 405.2 (El Salvador). Note that, Chile's and Cuba's areas are reduced to zero, practically. (Belize, Guyana, Suriname and FR. Guiana do not belong to Latin America).

### 3.3. Local and Global Distortions of the U.S. Map with Different Levels of Coarse-Graining for the Homicide Rates

Diffusion-based cartograms can be used to represent statistical variables at local and global levels. To carry this out, it is necessary to change, in different ways, the starting density $\rho_0(\vec{r})$ for the map to equalize and thus control the properties of the resulting cartogram, including a balance between accurate density equalization and readability (see Section 2). A very fine level of coarse-graining for $\rho_0(\vec{r})$ not only generates a more accurate representation of the statistical variable but also substantial local distortions of the map. In cartogram 8 (b), we show the homicide rates of the northeast region of the U.S. with a moderate coarse-graining, dividing the state's areas according to their population into metropolitan statistical and nonmetropolitan regions (see map 8 (a) without distortions). Metropolitan and nonmetropolitan areas are proportional to their homicide rates. For most of the states, the metropolitan areas show higher homicide rates than the nonmetropolitan areas.

Ultimately, in Figure 9 the homicide rate of continental U.S. (without Alaska) and that of Latin American countries are compared. The lowest homicide rate in Latin America is 3.09 (Chile), whereas the highest one is 405.2 (El Salvador). Due to this large difference, a highly distorted and unreadable cartogram is built whether country's areas are proportional to their homicide rates. A coarser homicide rate, averaging on large regions will cause less distortion, resulting in a map with features that are easier to recognize, but will give a less accurate impression of the true homicide rate distribution. Then, in cartogram 9, $\rho_0(\vec{r}) = (HomicideRate)_{country}$ is directly assumed, i.-e., the change in area (relative to a geographically accurate representation) is proportional to each country's homicide rate. The grayscale shading reflects homicide rates for each country at a logarithmic scale because of the aforementioned large difference between these values. Thus, the countries represented in this cartogram are still recognizable in spite of the distortions. The southern and northern countries are reduced with respect to their original sizes whereas Central America and the north of South America, in which there are higher homicide rates, are clearly enlarged.

# 4. Conclusion

Diffusion cartograms are an instructive and very useful tool to show statistical data including geographic information. The use of different mathematical estimations is really necessary to establish relationships between statistical data, but these relationships must be presented clearly without losing the main information one wants to transmit. By providing meaningful visualization statistical data, diffusion cartograms help transmit the desired information and also arouse the interest in a given topic. This technique can certainly improve the communication and outreach of statistical results to both specialized and unspecialized audiences. In this chapter, we study the homicide rates of the U.S., resorting to the goodness of diffusion cartograms. For instance, by means of cartogram 1(b) showing the homicide rates of the U.S., it is easy to recognize that the southern and center regions have higher rates than the northeastern and northwestern regions.

Cartograms not only make problem areas more readily apparent, but they also allow a glimpse into what may contribute to higher homicide rates. The homicide count is notably higher in more populated regions and vice versa, whereas the homicide rate does not follow this rule. We show that the homicide rate is linearly uncorrelated with the population. Instead, we found a weak correlation between homicide rates and the logarithm of the population. This correlation was put in evidence in a diffusion cartogram, in which large deformations of the map associated with high homicide rates agree with high values of the logarithm of population and vice versa, though there are exceptions due to the weakness of the correlation (see Figure 2(b)).

Strong correlations were found between homicide rates and other demographic, social, and economic variables, namely, robbery and aggravated assault rates, percentage of murders with firearms and a moderate correlation with the Human Development Index (HDI) was found. Cartograms 5(b) 6(b) and 7(b) convey these correlations and are similar between them.

Diffusion-based cartograms can be used to represent statistical variables at local and global levels. The method to build them allows one to keep a balance between good density equalization and low distortion of map regions, making it flexible enough for a wide variety of applications. A cartogram of the northeastern region of the U.S. with a moderate coarse-graining was built, in which the homicide rates are generally higher in the metropolitan areas. Finally, using a coarser grain, by means of a cartogram, we also compared the homicide rates of the U.S. with that of Latin America, evidencing a low value of the former with respect to that of the Latin American countries.

# References

[1] J. Candia, M. C. González, P. Wang, T. Schoenharl, G. Madey, A.-L. Barabasi, Uncovering individual and collective human dynamics from mobile phone records. *J. Phys. A: Math. Theor.* 41, 224015 (2008).

[2] R. Lambiotte, V. Blondel, C. de Kerchove, E. Huens, C. Prieur et al., Geographical dispersal of mobile communica- tion network. *Physica A* 387, 5317 (2008).

[3] D. Crandall, L. Backstrom, D. Cosley, A. Suri, D. Huttenlocher et al., Inferring social ties from geographic co- incidences. *Proc. Nat. Acad. Sci.* 107, 22436 (2010).

[4] B. Sanders, Seeing the quantum world. *Physics World* 21(12) (2008).

[5] M. Subba Rao, M. Aragon-Calvo, A picture of the cosmos. *Physics World* 21(12) (2008).

[6] C. Hidalgo, Thinking outside the cube. *Physics World* 21(12) (2008).

[7] A. Appel, C.J. Evangelisti, A.J. Stein, Animating quantitative maps with cellular automata. *IBM Tech. Dis. Bull.* 26, 953 (1983).

[8] D. Dorling, *Area Cartograms: Their use and creation, concepts and techniques in modern geography (CATMOG)*, No. 59 (Univ. of East Anglia, Norwich, U.K., 1996).

[9] S.M. Gusein-Zade, V.S. Tikunov, A new technique for con- structing continuous cartogram. *Cartogr. Geogr. Inf. Syst.* 20, 167 (1993).

[10] C.J. Kocmoud, Constructing continuous cartograms: a constraint-based approach. *Master's Thesis*, Texas A&M Visualization Laboratory, Texas A&M University, College Station, 1997.

[11] M. T. Gastner, M. E. J. Newman, Diffusion-based method for producing density-equalizing maps. *Proc. Nat. Acad. Sci.* 101, 7499 (2004).

[12] FBI's Web site: www.fbi.gov. Accessed 20 Sep. 2015.

[13] E.D. Gould, B.A. Weinberg, D.B. Mustard, Crime rates and local labor market opportunities in the United States: 1979-1997. *Rev. Econ. Stat.* 84, 45 (2002).

[14] D.T. Altindag, Crime and unemployment: evidence from Europe. *Int. Rev. Law Econ.* 32(1), 145-157 (2012)

[15] C.E. Moody, T.B. Marvell, On the choice of control variables in the crime equation. *Oxf. Bull. Econ. Stat.* 72, 696 (2010).

[16] A. Cotte Poveda, Economic development, inequality and poverty: an analysis of urban violence in Colombia. *Oxf. Bull. Econ. Stat.* 39, 453 (2011).

[17] C. Detotto, E. Otranto, Cycles in crime and economy: leading, lagging and coincident behaviors. *J. Quant. Criminol.*

[18] The United States Census Bureau (USCB). USCB's Web site: http://www.census.gov. Accessed 30 Aug. 2015.

[19] G. J. Privitera, *Statistics for the Behavioral Sciences*, $2^{nd}$ Ed. (SAGE Publications Inc., Washington DC, 2015).

[20] K. I. Mazzitello, J. Candia, Diffusion-Based Density-Equalizing Maps: an Interdisciplinary Approach to Visualizing Homicide Rates and Other Georeferenced Statistical Data, *Braz. J. Phys.* 42, 1-8, DOI 10.1007/s13538-012-0091-0 (2012).

[21] UNODC's Web site: www.unodc.org. Accessed 20 Sep. 2015.

In: Law Enforcement and Crime
Editor: Emanuel T. Rhodes
ISBN: 978-1-63484-127-6


*Chapter 6*

# JUSTIFYING VIOLENCE IN AMERICAN POPULAR CULTURE USING THE EXAMPLE OF 1987'S ROBOCOP

***Joanna Bogusławska*** *
Faculty of Philology, The University of Gdańsk,
Gdynia, Poland

## ABSTRACT

The following essay is an attempt to show that violence in American popular culture can be justified, and may even serve the story. What is to be analyzed in the given text is Paul Verhoeven's 1987 film Robocop. This essay will focus on depicting concrete scenes, and proving that apart from showing violence, they actually raise important sociological and psychological matters.

**Keywords**: Robocop, Murphy, popular culture, pop culture, violence, American, 1987

Popular culture is omnipresent; there is no doubt about it. It is obvious that due to its popularity, it is the source of trends and behavior patterns, it creates fashion, and it has basically every possible impact on its recipients. Children

* E-mail: joanna_boguslawska@wp.pl

and younger kids like to imagine they are the superheroes from their favorite comics or action movies, teenagers imitate their idols' hairstyles and the way they dress, and adults like to have gadgets referencing their beloved characters or artists. This is normal, and popular culture phenomena usually live intense but short lives because audiences are fussy and always looking for newer and more interesting superstars.

Before I get to analyzing the problem of violence in American popular culture, I believe it is crucial to establish what exactly popular culture is and what rules govern it.

The most common definition of pop culture is the one that can be found on www.dictionary.reference.com, which is:

> "Cultural activities or commercial products reflecting, suited to, or aimed at the tastes of the general masses of people."

Such a definition is general and quite imprecise, just like the analyzed phenomenon itself. Popular culture is a rather vague concept, and the question needs to be asked if something aimed at the tastes of the general masses is in fact culture in the first place. What is more, the term "general masses" might prompt pejorative associations, as it might describe a non-demanding audience, lacking taste and blindly following other people's expectations. Such a connotation involves a rather unfair perception of popular culture, and devaluates its role as a notion of culture.

The truth is that popular culture, being present in the world for decades, has created some classical phenomena itself. Its omnipresence in whatever we do or see and wherever we go makes it quite difficult for people to follow today's world if they don't know Homer Simpson, Madonna, or Superman. In movies and TV series, there are uncountable examples of jokes based on pop culture and tributes paid to it. People who do not know particular pop culture themes might have problems in decoding certain scenes, influences, and references.

Because English is the international lingua franca, it is obvious that the works created in this language stand a much bigger chance of being successful around the world, hence the domination of American pop culture. One might even encounter the term "homogenization of culture", i.e., its standardization according to a specific and popular formula. This is not necessarily bad, especially if we treat popular culture as a product that ought to be sold.

John Storey, in his book "Cultural Theory & Popular Culture: An Introduction," underscores the fact that there is no way to discuss pop culture without giving it a proper definition. He cites Raymond Williams, and proposes three different definitions. One describes culture as a source of intellectual, spiritual, and aesthetic development, and focuses on philosophers and thinkers. The second one revolves around the way people live (in a specific historical period, for example), and may concentrate on traditions, celebrations, and religions. The third definition focuses on culture's achievements, such as literature, opera, film, etc. Pop culture, according to Storey, is a blend of the latter two. In his book, he enlists certain categories characteristic of popular culture:

1. It is the culture known by the masses: not just a certain part of a society, but people around the world.
2. It does not fulfill high culture standards, and is made only to satisfy the masses, and for consumer reasons. This is a deeply pejorative description.
3. It is the culture that is based on what the people, its receivers, need and want.
4. It is the culture of rebellion, and of breaking the rules. It is poised against the stiff protocol that high culture ought to follow. It has no boundaries, and a limitless capacity that allows it to mix high and low culture together.

Since popular culture is a product aimed at being sold, it touches upon controversial, and quite often uncomfortable, matters on a daily basis. That is its nature: to pull cultural strings in order to create buzz and interest. Two things which seem to regularly cause pandemonium among popular culture's recipients, and instantly gain their attention, are sex and violence.

As far as sex is concerned, it is very often used to popularize artists. Madonna, for example, has been known for building interest around herself using scandalous behavior and provocative video-clips throughout her entire career. Once we recall the never-ending discussion around Miley Cyrus' infamous 2013 MTV Awards performance, we can see that this pattern is far from becoming outdated.

Sex as a pop-cultural way of gaining interest can have a meaningful educational overtone; nobody can deny popular culture's role in familiarizing people with gay relationships, women's sexual nature, and people's sexual needs in general. Apart from generating scandals and interest around artists and their work, there is no doubt that the presence of sex in mass media has had a positive influence on its recipients' awareness of these matters.

The other theme which is very often exploited in popular culture is violence, and unfortunately in this case, it can also have an impact on the reality in which we live. It is not dangerous when the actions it inspires cannot be taken seriously (for example, the fashion of biting people's necks, which appeared with the popularity of vampire-themed films and TV series), but when "Dexter" fans keep their fingers crossed for a main character who is a psychotic killer, one starts to wonder if the violence is going too far. In 2012, in Aurora, Colorado, James Eagan Holmes made himself up as the Joker, Batman's legendary foe in the DC Comics universe, and opened fire in a movie theater during a midnight screening of "The Dark Knight Rises". He killed 12 people and wounded over 70 others. The 1999 Columbine High massacre was swiftly blamed on Marilyn Manson's music, even though it has never been officially confirmed that the teenaged murderers were fans of the band. Video games have had a gloomy reputation as a violence-causing medium since the 1980s.

Since popular culture reaches masses, it is difficult for creators to restrain their imaginations and self-censor their work in case anyone interprets it the wrong way, or uses it as a source of inspiration for violent and extreme behavior. However, provided movie theaters pay attention to films' ratings, and video game sellers respect the age warnings on game boxes in order to protect young and immature people from watching a violent film or playing a bloody videogame, can violence in popular culture be justified? Can it serve a particular purpose?

What if violent scenes in a movie stand behind an important message, and are used not for the purpose of violence itself, but in order to force viewers to pay attention to certain things? What if they use particular models of behavior as a warning, as a wake-up call, or as a gruesome satire reflecting society's destructive tendencies?

The movie on which I want to base my analysis of the phenomenon of violence in American popular culture is Paul Verhoeven's 1987 film Robocop, an ultra-violent science-fiction motion picture which incorporates brutality in order to tackle much more serious problems and themes of the world we are all living in. The story of cyborg police officer Alex J. Murphy touches upon matters such as consumerism, corporations, violence, capitalism, and religion in the modern United States of America, and its dramatic and ironic conclusion is that a cyborg—half-man, half-machine—is the most human character in the film.

Robocop is set in a future Detroit that has gone bankrupt (!) and is now in the corporate hands of Omni-Consumer Products, known as OCP. OCP controls everything, from health services to the police. Just imagine: one company making decisions that concern absolutely every aspect of citizens' lives. A pretty dramatic vision, isn't it? Crime in Detroit is no longer a problem, but a true epidemic (as OCP's chairman says in one of the very first scenes in the film "Old Detroit has a cancer. That cancer is crime."), and the understaffed, underequipped, and underpaid police want to go on strike. However, OCP officials do not care about the possibility of having Detroit completely terrorized by gangsters. First of all, they want to tear it down and build a completely new city on the ruins. Secondly, they have already started building armed robots, ED-209s, which officially have been designed to patrol Detroit's dangerous cities and thus help the police; but unofficially, the corporation is already negotiating lucrative contracts with the military to build and sell ED-209s to them. Robots never get sick, and are not interested in paid leave or insurance. The police strike ends up being very convenient for OCP, because as it turns out, apart from the ED program, there is also the Robocop program, which intends to build police cyborgs. These are also intended to be sold to the army as a perfect combination of the intellect of the human brain, and the strength and precision of a machine. Due to ED-209's horrible malfunction, the Robocop program receives the chairman's acceptance, and the only thing the OCP needs now is a body: a police officer's body.

The setting of Old Detroit is dystopian. Everything is wrong here, and the rampant violence completes the image of a city running blindly towards self-destruction. It is well-known that Detroit used to be an American blue-collar capital, flourishing thanks to the automobile industry, but due to the manufacturing decline in the second half of the twentieth century, Detroit is depicted in the movie as living in the shadow of its own history, and is so weak it cannot even protect its citizens against crime and poverty.

In this essay, by using Robocop as an example, I have decided to show that violence in a pop-cultural movie can be justified, and although it is often very difficult to watch, it serves to show the viewers something much more important than the violence itself. Robocop proves that violence can allow the moviemakers to show values (or a lack of them), despair, corruption, consumerism, emotions, and drama. Perhaps the way it is all presented in Paul Verhoeven's film is controversial, but the impact those scenes have on viewers does not allow anyone who watches the movie to be indifferent to what they see. The violence in Robocop is horrible, bloody, and over the top, but completely essential to the film's structure and tone. It fits the characters, and is very much expected in the brutal environment the citizens of Detroit are used to, which is extremely violent, with no moral standards, soaked with corruption, and filled with crime.

I have selected six of the most brutal scenes, in my opinion, from Robocop, and will do my best to prove the scenes are about much more than just violence.

1. Officer down. Alex Murphy's last patrol.

Alex J. Murphy is transferred to a police station in the center of Detroit, and with his new partner, Officer Anne Lewis, they are patrolling the neighborhood. At one point they are told to chase a gang after a robbery. The scene shows Murphy as a devoted police officer, who, despite being obviously outnumbered, decides that he and Lewis are to continue the chase. It shows his determination; he is so focused on arresting the gang members, he decides not to wait for backup.

In the meantime, we can see Clarence Boddicker's gang inside a truck. Boddicker has no second thoughts about shooting one of his members, Bobby, and throwing his body on the police car right behind them just to slow down the pursuit. At this moment it is obvious that Boddicker has no allegiance, and no morals. However, it is what happens afterwards that truly shows the viewers that the gang members are devoid of any traces of humanity and conscience.

Alex Murphy's death is without a doubt the most violent scene in Robocop. The level of violence inflicted on one person is shocking; not only does the Boddicker group sadistically murder the officer, and not only do they enjoy torturing him, but they humiliate him, both as a police officer and as a human being, while doing so.

This scene, being so horrible and terrifying, serves to show the dehumanized world of Old Detroit, and it is the best way for a viewer to enter the extremely dangerous environment the characters of the film live in every day. What is more, this extremely brutal act of violence serves to give birth to another violent character, a vengeful ghost who will not stop until he finds and kills the people who robbed him of his life and humanity. Officer Murphy is an honest, brave, likeable character, and a loving and caring father and husband, and from the moment he is killed in the most brutal way possible by a group of cruel sociopaths, the viewers expect Boddicker's gang to face the same fate. There is no room for forgiveness; everyone wants Robocop to track them down and avenge his tragedy.

The violence in this scene builds the character and the pace of the film. It is necessary in order to understand why the rest of the movie is as brutal as it is, and it also builds the viewers' positive feelings towards the cyborg who, although not born yet, is obviously going to be more human than the criminals who deprived him of his life.

2. "Put down your weapon. You have 20 seconds to comply."

During the presentation of a robot who is supposed to support the police force (and earn some money for OCP), one of the company's board members is horribly killed by ED-209. The robot's malfunction is obviously an error, but the way the executive is gunned down—mercilessly, brutally, his body basically mangled by a machine gun—is beyond description. It is interesting to see the rest of the board members' reaction to what happened: nobody cares about the victim, and nobody is concerned that the man was killed, but everyone is disgusted by the mess in the conference room and angry that ED-209's malfunction will slow the robot program down. Dick Jones, the ED program coordinator sees the whole situation only as an embarrassment, nothing more than a glitch, and is very frustrated that the malfunction happened in front of the CEO. The excessive force displayed by ED-209 does not faze him or anyone else in the room. At this moment, Bob Morton, the chief engineer behind the Robocop program, sees this opportunity to gain OCP's CEO's attention and get money for his research. Bob Morton also does not care about the fact that a man was just brutally killed in front of him; he tidies himself (he spent the time of the shooting under a conference table), and immediately thinks of how he might benefit from the situation.

ED-209's malfunction sets the tone and legacy for OCP executives throughout the movie with just one scene. Human life has no worth. Welcome to Old Detroit.

3. "Thank you for your cooperation. Good night."

After all the Robocop tests are successful, the cyborg is assigned to Alex Murphy's police station and is soon sent to the streets to serve and protect the citizens of Detroit. During his very first night as a police officer, he has to deal with a shop robbery, a rape attempt, and a hostage crisis in the city hall.

Robocop's very first intervention is capturing a man who raids a small shop run by people in their sixties. As the robber threatens to shoot the woman behind the counter, "the new sheriff in town" (as Bob Morton calls Robocop) enters the store and knocks the bandit down.

Later on, he saves a woman who is about to be brutally raped by two men. During the first intervention in the supermarket, Robocop does not even need to use his gun, as the robber, apart from his dangerous looks, is not a real threat to anyone around him. However, since the woman is about to be used as a shield during the arrest, Robocop is forced to use his gun and shoots one of the attackers. When the woman comes to thank him, he only mentions she needs psychiatric help due to the stress she has been through; at this stage, Robocop has not recalled his humanity yet, and does not feel compassion or sympathy towards her. He is capable only of responding in the way his program allows him to.

The third intervention is a hostage crisis at city hall. Robocop walks into the building and swiftly disarms a dangerous man holding the people hostage. He does not negotiate, and he does not contact or warn the man that he is coming to get him; he simply acts. Again, a machine is programmed only to follow orders, in this case, to arrest the man breaking the law.

These three situations are not very brutal, but they show a police officer who is not afraid, who takes action, and who cannot be stopped. This is the kind of law enforcement the people of Old Detroit have hoped for, and soon they start believing he might save the city from the crime plague. What is really interesting in those three scenes is that they show Robocop almost as a classic western character. Here we have a lonely sheriff whose aim is to restore law and order in his city, who takes his gun out of a holster hidden on his hip and later on twirls it in his fingers before putting it back (a gesture very similar to the way Wild West gunslingers would do it), who works alone, who is alienated in his quest for restoring the law. The movie is basically a revisionist western that takes the classic themes of the genre and repurposes them. Robocop is the classic western lawman coming to clean up the town.

It is important to underscore the fact that at this point Robocop does not kill. He disarms his opponents, but uses force only up to the degree of neutralizing them. Things begin to change once Robocop becomes haunted by Murphy's memories.

## 4. "Murphy. It's you."

Once Alex Murphy's memories begin to emerge in Robocop's head, the cyborg's actions change dramatically. First of all, Officer Anne Lewis hints at what his real name is, and a later encounter with one of his murderers forces

Robocop to search for information about who he was in his human life. He discovers his real name, visits the house he used to live in with his family, and from that moment on, his second life as a machine begins to fade away. At that point, he becomes a human trapped in a robotic body, and is focused entirely on vengeance, and tracking down the people who took everything he loved away from him.

Robocop's raid on the drug factory, where Clarence Boddicker and some members of his gang are, also reflects classic western themes seen while watching classics like High Noon: a single law-abiding sheriff comes alone after the criminals. Despite bullets ricocheting off his armor, he firmly goes step by step into the warehouse, and systematically eliminates the gang members one by one, showing the criminals of Old Detroit exactly as much remorse as they show each other. It is no longer the Robocop trying to catch them harmlessly; his only warning is "Come quietly, or there will be trouble!" Robocop walks inside of the building in order to kill the gang members, and to search for Boddicker to arrest him and bring him to justice for what he had done to Alex Murphy. At one point, once he catches Boddicker and tightens his mechanical palm around his throat, visibly considering killing the gang leader, a glimpse of humanity appears in his head and he decides to take him to the police station instead, according to his directives. He follows procedure and upholds the law (probably one of the very last citizens of Old Detroit to do so). In this scene, Robocop's humanity has the face of revenge, revenge that the viewers have been keeping their fingers crossed for since officer Murphy's horrific death.

From this moment on, Robocop becomes a reflection of the world he lives in. Remembering what was done to him, he starts displaying the same lack of morals as the Old Detroit gangs he fights with. The warehouse scene is brutal, but it is a crucial moment for the story: Robocop the cyborg is fading away and Officer Alex Murphy is coming back. Now, the story becomes personal.

5. "I had to kill Bob Morton because he made a mistake. Now it's time to erase that mistake."

Once Clarence Boddicker is incarcerated, Murphy goes to the CEO headquarters in order to arrest Dick Jones. Robocop's investigation proves that Jones is a corrupt executive who controls Old Detroit's gun trade. He's also the mastermind behind Boddicker's gang. Murphy fails to arrest him, because one of his prime directives doesn't allow him to handcuff any of OCP's high executives. Dick Jones unleashes ED-209 to kill Robocop, but after seeing his robot malfunction again, he calls the police and orders them to gun down Murphy. The scene in which Robocop clumsily tries to protect himself against the cannonade is especially violent and uncomfortable. Here's Murphy again, fighting for his life, defenseless, and crawling on the floor, trying desperately to escape. The viewers have no choice but to feel sorry for the robot who doesn't understand why he's being shot at, and instinctively and hopelessly exposes his will to live. This is Old Detroit. It is not humans that the viewers feel sorry for; humans are exposed as corrupt, disgusting creatures. Viewers feel sorry for Murphy, now trapped in a mechanical body without his consent, built to obey the corporation he hated as a human, the only police officer in the city truly devoted to fighting crime, now being mercilessly shot at by his own fellow officers. This scene is not gory, and there's no blood, only sparks that appear when the bullets ricochet off of Robocop's body, but the emotional impact of it cannot be overestimated.

6. "They'll fix you. They fix everything."

After all the evil Clarence Boddicker has done, it is obvious that towards the end of the film, Robocop will finally confront his murderers. Just before the finale starts, Robocop, with Officer Lewis's help, comes to terms with what was done to him. He takes off his helmet, looks at his face for the first time, and finds out about what happened to his family. It is clear that he will take Boddicker and his crew down, and that this time nothing will stop him. What's symbolic about this scene is that Alex Murphy is accompanied by Anne Lewis. The two of them are going to face Boddicker's gang once again, alone and without any backup. Lewis helping her partner certainly allows her to clear her conscious, since it is mostly due to her mistakes that Murphy is killed at the beginning of the movie.

The deaths of the gang members are, basically, revolting. To call them brutal is simply not enough. Emil, one of the most violent members of the gang, literally melts after crashing into a toxic waste dump. Boddicker hits him with his car, and thus Emil's agony is over. His transformation and death comprise the most grotesque scenes of the film, and one of the only moments that actually shocks other characters. After killing all other members of the group, Murphy goes head to head with Clarence Boddicker, and is about to shoot him when he becomes trapped under a pile of scrap. Clarence sees it as an opportunity to kill the cyborg, and plunges a piece of metal straight through Robocop's armor. Murphy's face grimaces in pain, but he manages to stab Boddicker's throat with a metal spike, and the extreme blood splash indicates the end of the criminal. Originally, Robocop was supposed to stab him in the eye, but it was obvious that this wouldn't pass through the censors, and if the movie got an X rating, its distribution and box office success would have been very limited. Thus, what happens to Clarence is suggested rather than shown, but Boddicker still dies in a truly gruesome way. This is the way he deserves to die after all the things he has done. His death is Alex Murphy's redemption, a chance to leave his human life behind, and a chance to move forward.

There is an ironic moment at the end of the scene as Robocop and Lewis lay wounded, having successfully battled the Boddicker gang. Anne admits she has been very badly shot. Robocop, getting up, calms her down by saying, "They'll fix you. They fix everything." However, Murphy is being sarcastic; at this point it is clear that "they"—the technocrats—cannot fix everything, and Robocop is sadly referring to how brutally he has been "fixed" by them.

The last person left to arrest is Dick Jones. Murphy walks into a conference room where the whole board of OCP is having a meeting, and shows everyone evidence that Jones killed Bob Morton. The ED-209 project supervisor takes the corporation's chairman hostage. Because Murphy's fourth directive prevents him from arresting any high-ranking executive at OCP, he cannot react to this until the CEO fires Dick Jones. At that point, in a violent end to a violent film, Robocop repeatedly shoots Jones until he finally falls out of the window of the OCP skyscraper. Here is the most significant thing: none of the board members witnessing this situation is shocked that one of them was just killed. Murphy's co-creator even gives him a thumbs up, and the OCP president only straightens his tie and calmly asks Robocop his name before the meeting is resumed. He also praises Murphy for a job well-done. It is all one last reminder, at the end of the movie, that Old Detroit is a city deprived of humanity and compassion.

Violence begets violence, and this is an omnipresent theme in Paul Verhoeven's movie. Characters die horrible, brutal deaths because they are brutal by nature. Violence is a plot device, and something that shocks, but that also points out certain tendencies and the terrifying reality Murphy lives in. Old Detroit is a demoralized city, very violent, and extremely brutal, but it also serves as a warning. Robocop cautions against technological dependency (all technological wonders in the movie fail: ED-209 malfunctions, and even Robocop cannot be controlled. Some of his human memories return—something which was never supposed to happen—and despite corporate attempts to create a flawless, obedient machine, OCP fails thoroughly), against a dehumanized world with no values, and even against the superficial media responsible for creating the reality around us.

The action in Robocop is often interrupted by an evening news report with a meaningful slogan "You give us three minutes and we'll give you the world!" immediately points out that the information is to be presented in a superficial way. The news program has hardly anything to do with "objectivity". Rather it serves its viewers OCP propaganda, and due to the extreme time compression, the newscasters have no problem with juggling between news. It all provokes audience reflection on an important contemporary issue: how the news reduces information to entertainment.

The role of the news in spreading violence and brutality across the world of the film cannot be overstated. We learn that in South Africa, the white government considers using nuclear weapons against the black insurrection, and the commercial break actually shows a family playing a new board game "Nuke'm", thus acting out their destructive fantasies. We also learn that the U.S. and Mexican governments work together to pacify a revolution in Acapulco, that the Detroit Police have gone on strike, and that a laser satellite has accidentally fired upon numerous points on Earth, causing rain and forest fires, and killing American ex-presidents in Santa Barbara (once again, the movie exposes the critique of technology, warning that the human belief of having control over it is delusional). A question needs to be asked: how can Old Detroit not be brutal if it is fed with non-stop violence?

According to imdb.com, Robocop was submitted to the Motion Picture Association of America twelve times before finally receiving an R rating. The movie proves that if violence in a film is used in order to provide a good narrative, then it simply works, and it can be justified. One of the reasons why Robocop has been so successful and, despite being shot over 25 years ago, is still considered relevant and topical and has new generations of fans, is that everything, including the extreme violence, is essential to the story. Paul Verhoeven's movie is an adult film that deals with adult issues.

Robocop is not just a science-fiction movie about robots running free on the streets of Old Detroit, trying to maintain law and order on its streets. Verhoeven initially rejected the screenplay, considering it to be "just an action script". He stated later that he said, "'This is just an action script, and I don't think I can do this.' And they emphasized that I was wrong, and I was stupid, and there was more at stake than that." Encouraged by his wife to give it a chance, on a subsequent reading he saw in it philosophical themes—Christian themes of death, resurrection, and redemption—and agreed to do the film. Robocop successfully combines many genres. It is obviously a science-fiction movie, but one can easily trace elements of dark comedy, action, and fantasy. It is a complex, dystopian story, brutally showing the problems of human alienation. It is hard to imagine such a murky, pessimistic story without violence.

## References


http://dictionary.reference.com/browse/popular+culture Web. 18.10.2013

http://www.imdb.com/title/tt0093870/trivia?ref_=tt_trv_trv Web. 20.10.2013

http://www.mlive.com/news/grand-rapids/index.ssf/2009/04/separating_myth_from_fact_on.html Web. 19.10.2013

http://www.nytimes.com/1987/07/24/movies/at-the-movies.html Web. 20.10.2013

http://www.salon.com/1999/09/23/columbine_4 Web. 19.10.2013

Robocop – Director's Edition, DVD, 2007, Metro Goldwyn Mayer

Storey J. Cultural Theory & Popular Culture. An Introduction. Edinburgh: Pearson Education Limited, 2006

# INDEX